THE GERMAN
EMPIRE

Modern Library Chronicles

MICHAEL STÜRMER

THE GERMAN EMPIRE

1870-1918

A MODERN LIBRARY CHRONICLES BOOK

THE MODERN LIBRARY

NEW YORK

2000 Modern Library Edition

Copyright © 2000 by Michael Stürmer

All rights reserved under International and Pan-American
Copyright Conventions. Published in the United States by
Random House, Inc., New York, and simultaneously in Canada
by Random House of Canada Limited, Toronto.

MODERN LIBRARY and colophon are registered trademarks
of Random House, Inc.

This work was originally published in Great Britain by
Weidenfeld & Nicolson, a division of
The Orion Publishing Group.

Cover photo: Kaiser Wilhelm II, 1910, by E. Bieber, AKG London

LIBRARY OF CONGRESS CATALOGING-IN-PUBLICATION DATA
Stürmer, Michael.
The German Empire, 1870–1918/Michael Stürmer.
p. cm.—(Modern Library chronicles book)
Includes bibliographical references and index.
ISBN 0-679-64090-8 (alk. paper)
1. Germany—History—1871–1918. 2. Germany—Social
conditions—1871–1918. 3. Germany—Foreign relations—
1871–1918. I. Title. II. Modern Library chronicles.
DD220.S79 2000
943.08—dc21 00-58745

Modern Library website address: www.modernlibrary.com

Printed in the United States of America on acid-free paper

2 4 6 8 9 7 5 3 1

ACKNOWLEDGMENTS

I wish to thank Sam Hudson, London, for his unfailing advice on matters of substance and style. I also wish to thank the rector and staff at the Wissenschaftskolleg zu Berlin (Institute for Advanced Study) for the most generous hospitality during a sabbatical in the academic year 1999–2000, providing inspiration, good company, and an environment of intellectual challenge. At the Friedrich Alexander–University of Erlangen, Institut für Geschichte, Monika Frielinghaus and Markus Freidrich provided much welcome help, from library services to advice on how to make computers conform to author's wishes.

CONTENTS

MAPS

PREFACE

In the ancient city of Koblentz where the Moselle flows into the Rhine there is, in front of the Romanesque church of St. Castor, a neoclassical fountain with a plaque. The inscription celebrates the passage of Napoleon's grande armée through the city en route to Russia to crush the Tsar's despotism. It is signed, "Jules Doazan, sous préfet de la ville de Coblentz." Underneath there is a second inscription which reads, "Vu et approuvé par nous le commandant Russe de la ville de Coblentz."* The first inscription is dated 1812, the second one 1813. This plaque encapsulates the German question.

Germany is situated at the heart of Europe where all the peninsulas and lands forming the European continent are linked to Eurasia. Germany, whether its citizens are aware of the fact or not, determines through its history and geography the destinies of most countries in Europe; and, in turn, the fate of Germany is, for better or for worse, of

* "Jules Doazan, prefect of the town of Koblentz." "Seen and approved by the Russian commander of the town of Koblentz."

the utmost importance for these countries. This has been the *conditio Germaniae* ever since Europe began to evolve a thousand years ago. Strategic and cultural interdependence made the Holy Roman Empire for many centuries the center of the European system, but far from being the imperial master of Europe's destinies, the German lands proved time and again to be a peacetime chessboard or a wartime arena for the competition of the European powers who were rising to modern statehood and sovereignty and fighting for influence. The German constitution, forever organized in an uneasy equilibrium between the Emperor and the territorial rulers, became more "Europeanized," and less nationalistic in outlook and intent: today's map of Europe, the result of the changes that took place in the 1990s—Germany unified within the framework of NATO followed by a quantum leap in European integration through economic and monetary union—is nothing but a modern and more enlightened variation upon a very old theme.

This book traces the rise and fall of the German Empire from its inception after the Franco-Prussian war of 1870 to its demise, in defeat and revolution, in 1918. Otto von Bismarck, its creator, put an end to the age-old European role of Germany by excluding the vast and unwieldy Habsburg lands. But even so the new German nation-state was, almost inevitably, a dramatic challenge to the established balance of power. "Europe has lost a mistress and won a master" was a complaint heard around London after France's defeat. Benjamin Disraeli, later the Earl of Beaconsfield, pointed out in the House of Commons in 1871 that this war—referring to the recent Franco-German war—was "a German revolution," and "a greater political event than the French revolution of last century. I don't say a greater, or as great a social event. What its social consequences may be, is in the future... there is not a diplomatic tradition which has not been swept away... What has really come to pass? The balance of power has been entirely destroyed." There was an ominous tone of warning in his analysis, and it was heeded by the contemporary generation of German leaders, especially by Bismarck—whose epithet of the "Iron" Chancellor disguised his heroic pessimism—and by his successor Count Caprivi. But by the end of the century the European stage had been superseded by a global one. The United States and Japan had become world powers in their own right and markets, resources, battle-fleets and sea-lanes had become vital components of national power and identity in Europe, Germany being no exception. And there was no longer Bismarck to sound the alarm.

Why did the Empire end in war? Was this, to put it into ancient Greek terms, nemesis following hubris? Were the inevitable stresses of transforming an agricultural society into an industrial one uncontainable? Or was Germany caught in its geography, its politicians blind to the troubling fact that the country was too big for the old balance of power to continue but too small to impose a new equilibrium? Was German militarism any worse than French chauvinism, Russian expansionism or British jingoism and imperialism? Perhaps Germany's sudden rise after centuries of defeat and suffering overtaxed the historical and strategic imagination of its power elites whose outlook and sensitivity to danger were essentially continental rather than global in reach. It was the industrialist Walther Rathenau who said, not long before the outbreak of World War I, that the Germans knew their map but were ignorant of the globe.

Within the lifetime of one generation Germany was able to become the foremost industrial and trading power in Europe. Bismarck's revolution from above unleashed vast energies through the nation state, not entirely unlike events in France eighty years before. Industrial performance was second to none and was accompanied by the birth of the welfare state and democratic institutions and aspirations; of a socialist subculture and an ambitious liberal bourgeoisie unsure of itself but driven by nervous energy and creative unrest. At the turn of the century the language of the sciences was, in many parts of the world, German. A vast number of Nobel prizes went to German scholars, many of them Jews. German big business and banks were probably organized more efficiently than most competitors except for the United States. German universities became the model for many establishments of higher education from Turkey to North America. If the French Impressionists dominated the art world in the nineteenth century, after the turn of the century German art movements became equally important. In literature it was probably the Germany of Gerhard Hauptmann, Thomas Mann or Theodor Mommsen, all of them Nobel Prize winners, that most sensitively expressed the drama and contradictions of industrial society. A letter which appeared in *The Times* in August 1914 under the heading "Scholars' Protest Against War" summed up a widely held view: "We regard Germany as a nation leading the way in the arts and sciences, and we have all learnt and are learning from German scholars."

However, ultimately, as has often been said, perhaps the Kaiser's rule was too authoritarian and out of touch to allow Germany to evolve into a more open society with more liberal politics. Perhaps World War I, in all its patent absurdity, was an inevitable result of Europe's reckless power play, with Germany at the center. It was a grave not only for millions of young men and their dreams but also for the liberal institutions that had nurtured the genius of nineteenth-century Europe. Alas, that genius was of the self-destructive kind. The war, for all its brutality, did bring with it the chance of female liberation and democratic transformation, but it turned out also to contain the seeds of totalitarian dictatorship.

CHRONOLOGY

Please note that some dates are approximate or speculative.

1848–49 Social and political revolutions throughout most of continental Europe. The German parliament convenes in Frankfurt's Paulskirche under pressure from the radical left as much as from the old guard. After the parliament adopts the "Little-Germany" concept (a nation-state excluding Austria), the Prussian king refuses the Imperial crown offered by the Frankfurt parliament. The liberal and democratic constitution drawn up there is never put into practice.

1852 Napoleon III becomes Emperor of France after a *coup d'état*.

1854–56 Crimean War. Great Britain, France and Piedmont-Sardinia go to war against Russia in the Crimean Peninsula to preserve the Ottoman Empire. Prussia is neutral, but pro-Russian. Peace of Paris. Russia surrenders her claim on the Ottoman Empire.

1859 Piedmont-Sardinia, supported by France under Napoleon III, goes to war against Austria. Prussia, Russia and Great Britain are neutral. The Prussian army is mobilized to put pressure on Austria.

1861–65 American Civil War. France sends troops to Mexico.

1862 William I makes Otto von Bismarck Prime Minister of Prussia.

1864 February–August: Prussia and Austria at war with the Kingdom of Denmark over national self-determination for the largely German-speaking provinces of Schleswig and Holstein. Condominium between Vienna and Berlin collapses. A promised referendum never takes place. After 1866 Schleswig-Holstein annexed by Prussia.

1866 April: Bismarck concludes a military alliance with Italy to prepare for war against Austria.

June–August: "the German War" between Prussia and Austria and the majority of the states of the German Confederation. Italy, on the side of Prussia, wins Lombardo-Venetia. After the battle of Königgrätz an armistice and preliminary peace are made at Nikolsburg. After the Peace of Prague the electorate of Hesse, the Grand Duchy of Nassau, the Free City of Frankfurt and the Kingdom of Hanover are annexed by Prussia.

1867 The North German Confederation is founded under Prussian hegemony. The constitution provides for democratic elections and a liberal parliament, but control of the administration and the army remain firmly in the hands of the "presidium," i.e., the King of Prussia. Bismarck becomes Prime Minister, foreign minister and chancellor.

1867–68 The Customs Union, comprising both northern and southern states, acquires a parliament and passes the liberal "Gewerbeordnung" ("trading regulation"), setting free market forces. The four German states south of the river Main are linked to Prussia through military integration. There is popular resentment in the south against Prussian domination.

1870–71 The Spanish Parliament offers the crown to a Prince from the Catholic, South German line of the Hohenzollern. King William of Prussia declines the offer, but Bismarck uses this to create a storm of French public opinion against Prussia and Napoleon III finds himself forced into war with Prussia and, by implication, the whole of Germany. After the surrender of the Imperial army, war is fought and lost by the Third French Republic. Uprising of the Commune of Paris.

January 1871: King William I of Prussia proclaimed German Emperor at Versailles.

May 1871: the Frankfurt Peace Treaty takes Alsace and Lorraine from France and demands five billion francs in reparations.

1871–72 Deutsche Bank and Dresdner Bank founded. German population at 41 million (as compared to 68 million in 1913).

1873 "Three Emperors' Alliance" is initiated by Bismarck to prevent war between Russia and Austria. *Kulturkampf* begins—a campaign of the State against the Church.

1874 Richard Wagner moves into Haus Wahnfried in Bayreuth.

1876 Nikolaus Otto invents the internal-combustion engine.

1876–77 Balkan wars: Serbia and Russia's battle against Ottoman Empire ends in Russian victory. The Tsar dictates the peace treaty of San Stefano.

1878 Bismarck calls the Congress of Berlin to settle the conflict between Great Britain and Russia over controls of the Eastern Mediterranean. Resentment in Russia against German interference on behalf of Austria-Hungary.

In Germany an anti-socialist law bans the Socialist party but allows them parliamentary representation. Socialists dissociate themselves from anarchism and terrorism.

First football club is founded in Hanover.

1879 Germany makes a dual alliance with Austria-Hungary to deter Russian attack and to stabilize the Balkans. Anglo-Russian confrontation over Afghanistan: conflict over territory in Asia at its height.

German agriculture comes under competitive pressure from the U.S. and Russia and Germany turns from her traditional free-trade policy to protectionism.

Siemens Company builds first electrical locomotive.

1881 Bismarck achieves a new secret "Three Emperors' Alliance" to last for three years.

A telephone network is launched in Berlin.

1882 Robert Koch develops antidote to tuberculosis. New colonial expansion of the European powers is led by Great Britain and France. In the following years Germany acquires colonies in east Africa and south-west Africa.

1884–85 Congo Conference in Berlin is called. To prevent major colonial confrontations boundaries are drawn to delineate spheres of influence between the great powers in Europe.

1886 Gottlieb Daimler and Carl Benz have their four-wheel cars patented.

1887 Emil Berliner develops the gramophone record-player. Heinrich Hertz discovers electrical waves.

1887–90 Germany makes a secret Reinsurance Treaty with Russia specifying both their neutrality should war break out with Russia or France.

1888 Hertz discovers the wireless telegraph, hence laying foundations for the invention of radio and television.

Emperor William I dies aged 88; Emperor Frederick III, suffering from cancer, dies after 100 days in power and is succeeded by William II, aged 28.

1889 Major strikes in the coalmines of the Ruhr area and in Upper Silesia.

Great Britain begins to modernize her naval battle-fleet.

April: Adolf Hitler is born in Braunau in Austria into the family of a customs official.

1890 March: Bismarck resigns after 28 years in power in Prussia and Germany.

Emil von Behring develops a serum against diphtheria and tetanus.

1890–94 Count Leo von Caprivi, a general, appointed chancellor on Bismarck's fall. He works with a center-left majority in the Reichstag. He exchanges with Great Britain Zanzibar for Heligoland in the North Sea, against heavy opposition from the nationalist right who have formed the Alldeutscher Federation. To help German export industries tariffs are considerably lowered in a trade agreement with Russia.

1891 A Franco-Russian military alliance is formed. Gerhard Hauptmann (winner of the Nobel prize for literature in 1912) writes *Die Weber*.

1894 Kaiser William II approves Admiral Tirpitz's plans for a completely modernized German battle fleet.

Caprivi is dismissed and Prince Hohenlohe becomes Chancellor.

1895 Sigmund Freud and Josef Breuer publish *Studien über Hysterie,* the first study of psychoanalysis.

1896 Otto Lilienthal dies in a crash in the glider that he invented.

1897 Foreign Secretary Bernhard von Bülow decides Germany's right to a colony "in the sun": the Kaiser travels to Istanbul, Baalbek and Jerusalem.

Preparations are made for the "Baghdad Railway"

planned to modernize the Ottoman infrastructure and expand German influence.

The first Zionist Congress is held in Basle.

1898–1901 Boer War in South Africa results in pervasive anti-British sentiment in Germany.

1900 A Civil Code is instituted for the first time in Germany.

The first Zeppelin flies.

1901 Alfred Nobel endows the Nobel Award: among the first four recipients are two Germans—Conrad Röntgen for physics and Emil von Behring for medicine.

Thomas Mann's *Die Buddenbrooks* is first published (and wins the Nobel Prize for literature in 1929).

1902 Robert Bosch develops the spark plug.

Historian Theodor Mommsen wins the Nobel Prize for literature.

1904 The *Entente Cordiale* is made between Paris and London, in the hope of containing German power and influence.

1904–5 War breaks out between Russia and Japan heralding the beginning of Japanese expansion in East Asia.

1905 Richard Strauss's *Salome* is first performed and Albert Einstein's *Theory of Relativity* is published.

The "Schlieffen Plan" is drawn up constituting a fatal narrowing of German strategic options. The strategy plans to mass the majority of the German army on the western front to force France to surrender, on the assumption the Russians will take at least six weeks to mobilize their troops on the Eastern Front.

1906 July: German attempts to reverse the Franco-Russian alliance fail at a meeting between the Tsar and the Kaiser at Bjoerkoe near St. Peterburg.

1908–9 Both Britain and Germany forced to find tax revenue to continue their respective Dreadnought battleship building programs. Lloyd George's "butcher" budget fails to do so and leads to constitutional crisis in Britain. Bülow also fails to raise the necessary funds, but a special tax on champagne remains.

October: Austria-Hungary annexes Bosnia and Herzegovina. The Russians are humiliated in defeat. Bülow announces a "Nibelungen loyalty" to Austria.

1909 Fritz Hofmann invents artificial rubber.

Theobald von Bethmann Hollweg becomes Chancellor.

1912 British War Secretary Lord Haldane visits Berlin to seek naval arms control in Germany. An Anglo-German agreement fails, but both powers cooperate in crisis management in the Balkans and prepare plans for dividing Portuguese colonies in case of Portugal's default.

April: the unsinkable *Titanic* hits an iceberg. In Munich the artists' group "der Blaue Reiter" ("the Blue Riders") is founded by, amongst others, Franz Marc, Paul Klee, Wassily Kandinsky, August Macke.

1912–13 Balkan wars: the smaller Balkan powers against the Ottoman Empire.

1913 As a response to the growing strength of French and Russian armies, Germany intensifies conscription.

Banque de France and Reichsbank inconspicuously withdraw gold from circulation.

1914 June: Archduke Franz Ferdinand, successor to the crowns of Austria and Hungary, is assassinated by a Serb-Bosnian terrorist while on an official visit in Sarajevo.

July: war breaks out.

August–September: all major European powers go to

war; German troops march through neutral Belgium towards Paris. German strategy fails in the west but in the east its troops block and reverse the Russian invasion. War begins in the trenches. Censorship is instituted and strikes are banned.

1914–15 Turkey and Bulgaria join the war on the side of the Central Powers: Japan and Italy on the side of the *Entente*.

1915 April: the Germans are the first to use gas in battle.

May: The sinking of the *Lusitania,* with many American citizens on board, brings U.S. closer to war with Germany.

1916 February–September: battle of Verdun. Losses on both sides come to 700,000.

December: all out mobilization of the population in Germany begins through "Vaterländisches Hilfsdienstgesetz" ("Patriotic Emergency Drafting"). In a *quid pro quo* trade unions become partners of management and government.

Central Powers offer peace negotiations; *Entente* powers refuse.

Kingdom of Poland proclaimed, under German influence.

1916–18 Third High Command under Paul von Hindenburg and Erich Ludendorff assumes informal dictatorial powers.

1917 February: the German admiralty announces the launch of unlimited submarine warfare, thus making U.S. intervention in the war almost inevitable. A revolution takes place in Russia. The moderate Aleksandr Kerensky becomes Prime Minister.

March: the Brusilov offensive fails: a dual winged attack by Russian troops into Vilna Naroch as a counter to

German activity in Verdun. The offensive grinds to a halt in the mud of the spring thaw.

April: the Kaiser's Easter message promises democratic reform.

July: in the Reichstag a center-left majority forms, the predecessor of the Weimar coalition of 1919, and comes out in favor of "peace without annexations and reparations."

November: furnished with money from the German High Command, Lenin and his band of Bolsheviks are allowed travel through German territory to stage a coup in St. Peterburg. The Russian front breaks down and civil war ensues. Lenin's message to his people offers peace through world revolution.

1918 January: the "Fourteen Points" are pronounced by President Wilson in a message to both Houses of Congress. They include national self-determination institution of the League of Nations, free trade and open diplomacy.

March: at Brest Litovsk a German peace in Eastern Central Europe is resolved: the Bolsheviks sign under the silent assumption that a German revolution is imminent and will enable them to recoup their losses.

June–July: on the Western front German troops stage last offensives which fail.

August: British tanks break through German lines at Amiens.

September: the German High Command demands a Parliamentary government be installed to offer armistice to *Entente* powers.

October–November: Chancellor Prince Baden heads a center-left coalition and initiates sweeping constitutional reform, offering an armistice to President Wilson on the basis of the "Fourteen Points." As parts of the German battle fleet receive orders for a last-stand battle in the North Sea, mutinies cripple the ships. Breakdown of western front; revolution throughout Germany begins. The Kaiser deserts to Holland; German princes resign; beginning of civil war in Germany. Karl Liebknecht, a Communist, and Philipp Scheidemann, a Social Democrat, compete to proclaim Germany a republic. Friedrich Ebert, leader of the Social Democrats, takes over from Prince Baden.

November: the armistice is signed at Compiègne, France.

1918–19 "Zentralarbeitsgemeinschaft" ("Central Working Community") is set up between industry and trade unions to transform revolution into social reform.

1919 January: elections throughout Germany give center-left sweeping majority. National Assembly convenes in the provincial security of Weimar.

June: Paris Peace Conference of 26 nations. Germany signs at Versailles, Hungary at Trianon, Austria at St. Germain, Turkey at Sèvres (in 1920). Russia is not represented. John Maynard Keynes of the British delegation warns the treaty contains "the seeds of the next war."

April: statute of League of Nations set up.

August: a constitutional compromise is reached in Weimar: "Verfassung des Deutschen Reiches" ("the constitution of the German Empire"). The Weimar Republic is born.

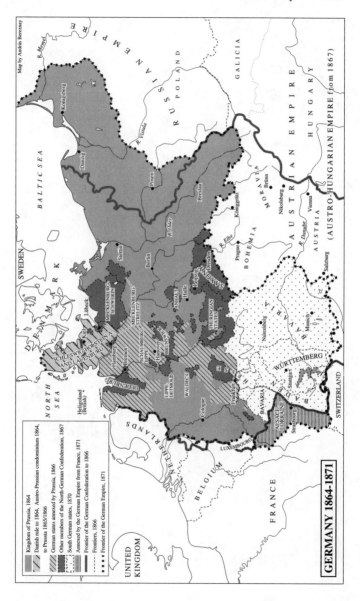

Map by András Bereznay

GERMANY 1864–1871

Kingdom of Prussia, 1864

Danish rule to 1864, Austro-Prussian condominium 1864, to Prussia 1865/1866

German states annexed by Prussia, 1866

Other members of the North-German Confederation, 1867

South German states, 1870

Annexed by the German Empire from France, 1871

Frontier of the German Confederation to 1866

Frontiers, 1866

Frontier of the German Empire, 1871

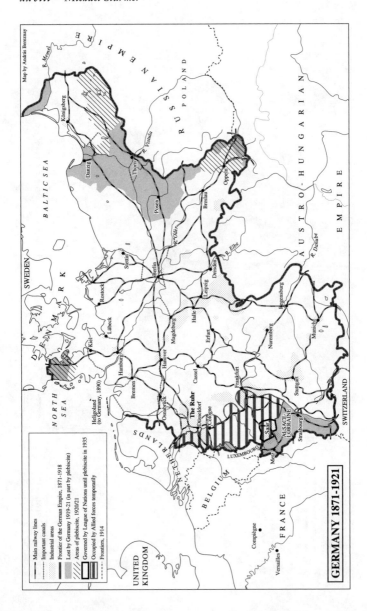

Map by András Bereznay

GERMANY 1871-1921

Main railway lines
Important canals
Industrial areas
Frontier of the German Empire, 1871-1918
Lost by Germany 1919-21 (in part by plebiscite)
Areas of plebiscite, 1920/21
Governed by League of Nations until plebiscite in 1935
Occupied by Allied forces temporarily
Frontiers, 1914

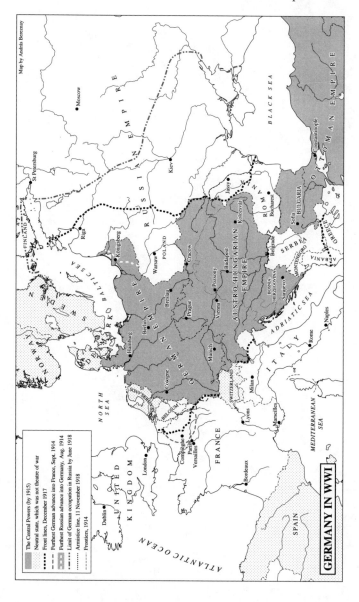

Map by András Bereznay

GERMANY IN WWI

The Central Powers (by 1915)
Neutral state, which was not theatre of war
Front lines, December 1917
Furthest German advance into France, Sept. 1914
Furthest Russian advance into Germany, Aug. 1914
Limit of German occupation in Russia by June 1918
Armistice line, 11 November 1918
Frontiers, 1914

THE GERMAN
EMPIRE

Prologue:

Imperial Birthday

The vast Palace of Versailles had not seen a gathering of such splendor for over fifty years. There were a few solemn elderly gentlemen in tailcoats, but the remainder of the throng were officers in victorious mood—uniformed, decorated, their left hands on their sword hilts, plumed helmets in their right. This was the flower of the German ruling aristocracy, with some senators from the three remaining Free Cities in northern Germany and a handful of Reichstag members, assembled to witness the proclamation of the last European empire on January 18, 1871.

Those versed in Roman history among the crowd could not fail to recall the brutal tag, *Exercitus facit imperatorem*—"the army makes the emperor." Versailles was, indeed, the camp of the German allies, united as never before by their victory over Napoleon III of France. The Galerie des Glaces where they stood might have been a hospital ward full of Prussian wounded a few weeks ago, and the war might be continuing against the republic that had succeeded the second Napoleonic Empire, but peace was on the way. It was bound to be bitter for France, losing Alsace and Lorraine and paying reparations of 5 billion gold francs to a part of Europe long regarded as her diplomatic playing field or chosen battleground. But it was also to be bitter for Germany: Bismarck soon learned that "France is impossible"—there could be no European system with a revengeful France; nor could there be one without it.

A vengeful France had gone to war in July 1870, much against the better judgment of Napoleon III, in order to stop Prussia, already dominant in Germany, from overawing Europe as well. "Revenge for Sadowa" had been the somewhat bizarre battle cry of the French press, Sadowa or Königgrätz being the place of the decisive Prussian victory over the Austrians in 1866. France had not participated in that war and had itself defeated Austria in 1859 in Italy, but parliament and the press in Paris regarded European hegemony as a French birthright since the days of François I. Unless Napoleon prevented Germany's seizure of this inheritance, he knew he would lose his throne. Surrounded at Sedan a few weeks later, together with most of his army, he lost it anyway.

It was a far-fetched idea, in the true meaning of that phrase, to proclaim the German Emperor at such a distance from home. It seemed also to add insult to injury, to use a building synonymous with the glory of France. But to have used Berlin would have exposed the apparently equal alliance for what it was, a Prussian military monarchy, and would have reminded Germans that the King of Prussia had, not long ago, been only one among the "seven pillars of the empire," the electors of the Emperor. Frankfurt was too much associated with the medieval Empire, as the Emperors' coronations had taken place in its Gothic cathedral. It was also associated with the troubling events of 1848, the "mad year" when all the thrones throughout

German lands were shaking at the threat of the people's sovereignty, when civil war raged in Berlin, Baden, Austria, Saxony and the Palatinate, and the new Emperor, then merely a Prussian Prince, had been forced to find a diplomatic pretext to travel in England. Moreover, Frankfurt, once the "Holy Roman Empire's bullion vault," had lost its status as a Free City only four years before, as punishment for siding with Austria in the brief military encounter of 1866. No one had forgotten how the rich cousins in the south had derided sandy Brandenburg, Prussia's power center, as "the Holy Roman Empire's pounce box"—the latter a device for sprinkling sand on a letter so as to dry the ink. Compared to the embarrassments waiting at home, Versailles seemed an almost rational choice. The actual day, January 18, had been chosen as the 170th anniversary of the self-styled coronation, defying the Holy Roman Emperor's prerogative, of Elector Frederick III as Frederick I "King in Prussia," in 1701.

Otto von Bismarck, Prussian Prime Minister and now German Chancellor, left nothing to chance, either in the conduct of politics or in the stage management of the ceremony. A formal coronation of King William of Prussia as German Emperor was out of the question. There was no imperial crown—and to the end of Germany's days as an empire there would never be one, except as an artist's impression on coins, flags, post-boxes and the like; neither was there anyone able or willing to put one on the King's head. A bishop? He himself was "supreme bishop" over all the Protestants throughout his lands. The precedent of Napoleon Bonaparte in 1804 was too overwhelming to allow him to crown himself. Besides, King William hated the whole business, which had been imposed on him by Bismarck. Educated to hold his Habsburg cousins in deep respect and to look with disdain on the mushroom growth of the two French Napoleonic empires, he had a deep aversion to seeing a similar title invented for himself. He used to call it a mere *Charaktermajor,* referring to the rank conferred on officers who actually retired as captains. When Bismarck greeted him on the morning of the 18th, rather like Mephisto to his Faustus, the old King observed, sadly, "Today we are carrying the old Prussia to its grave." Bismarck could have replied that, after the recent strong injection of democracy into the body politic, after the alliance made with the moneyed classes and the advances made to the proletariat, old Prussia was doomed anyway. Had His Majesty forgotten 1848, or that only a few years ago he had been locked in a bitter struggle with his own parliament? It was certainly not of Bismarck's choosing that he was now riding the wild horses of modern nationalism.

As instructed by Bismarck, the Grand Duke of Baden stepped forward to cry "Long Live Emperor William," swords were drawn—quite dangerous given the crowd—and the Emperor was installed. One person conspicuous by his absence was King Ludwig of Bavaria, second only to the new Emperor in power and precedence. Ludwig's reputation for mental instability and homosexuality meant that Bismarck was quite happy that he had not taken the trouble to come to Versailles. Ludwig had in any case already performed the one vital task that Bismarck required of him—to send a letter, drafted of course by Bismarck, to the King of Prussia, asking him to become Emperor. Bismarck knew that one of Ludwig's more expensive passions was palace building, something much appreciated by today's tourists as they view Herrenchiemsee, Hohenschwanstein, and Linderhof, but not by the Bavarian parliament and treasury at the time. The reward

Bismarck proffered for Ludwig's letter was 5 million thaler, in cash if desired. The money was procured from secret funds derived from the wealth of the deposed King of Hanover, who, like the King of Bavaria, had been unwise enough to back Austria against Prussia in 1866. Bismarck's lavish bribe meant that the palaces continued to rise among the Bavarian lakes and mountains, and Ludwig could continue to underwrite the expensive ideas of his favorite composer, Richard Wagner. It was not until after World War I, when the empire that these payments had facilitated was no more, that this transaction was revealed.

The German "Reich," or empire, put on the map of Europe by the kingdom of Prussia, was the very antithesis to the pre-modern, supra-national empire of the past millennium. The old empire had been a republic under a ruler elected during the last 500 years of its existence almost invariably from the house of Habsburg. The English or French translation of "empire," especially after the brutal rise and hellish fall of the "third Reich," is misleading with its implications of aggression. The medieval Reich was a conglomerate of spiritual and temporal powers: of princes, bishops, free cities like Hamburg or Frankfurt, and various other autonomous components. Its legitimacy derived from its claim to be a continuation of the Roman Empire. It was not a precursor of the modern dynastic state let alone the nation-state of the nineteenth century. The Lutheran translation of the *pater noster* mentions the Reich twice, meaning God's kingdom. But the vastness of the term corresponded to the looseness of its organization and the undetermined nature of where it began and where it ended. Worse still, after Napoleon the Holy Roman Empire was no more and the term emperor was no longer associated with the largely impotent and ceremonial authority of the Habsburgs but with his military usurpation of revolutionary power. Therefore, resurrecting the title with its controversial history was inevitably a gamble, putting the new Germany into the ambit of two traditions mutually incompatible and open to dangerous interpretation.

The emperor's title and the name of empire promised the Germans much more than Bismarck, returning after 1871 to his conservative beginnings, was willing to allow, let alone deliver. He had fought, and won, the war of 1866 against Austria—the first victory of the future German Empire—precisely in order to cut Germany down to a more acceptable size. The Germany confirmed through the victory over imperial France in 1870 was to be, once the era of war was over, a pillar of stability, and all of Bismarck's subsequent policy was directed to that one great goal. The Germany Bismarck designed and put on the map was a greater Prussia in the guise of the German nation-state, much rather than an expanding empire. But given the dynamism of the industrial age and the rise of the middle classes and the proletariat, Germany could not, as Bismarck would have wished, remain an island of tranquility and social equilibrium in a sea of world-wide imperialism and the German empire finally lived up to its mistaken name. The ceremony at Versailles in the icy mirrored gallery of the Sun King, had given a deceptive seal of finality to an ongoing and unstoppable revolution which in turn was part of a world-wide change. In this vast transformation Germany was to be an ever more important player. But the post-Bismarck German establishment was inexperienced and unable to accept the fact that, in order to survive, they must be the guardians and not the challengers of the balance of power.

1

GERMAN ANGST, GERMAN HOPE

There had always been a notion that the tribes between the North Sea and the Alps shared not only their geographic space, but also their language and basic concepts of law. However, the lands forming the ancient Reich, the Holy Roman Empire from the Middle Ages to the era of the French Revolution and Napoleon were never clearly defined. Until the Peace of Westphalia in 1648, concluding the Thirty Years War, they had even extended to the Swiss cantons and the Dutch provinces. Before the age of the nation state a number of foreign rulers, such as the King of Sweden who controlled the coastal lands of the Baltic, or the King of Denmark who held the territories of Schleswig and Holstein, possessed rights and lands in Germany and ruled over German-speaking populations. The German-speaking lands of central Europe were not a nation-state in the making, unlike early modern Britain or France, Spain or Sweden, which were hammered together by a powerful dynasty like the Tudors or the Bourbons, long before the nation-state made its appearance in modern Europe. The Holy Roman Empire, "das Reich," was rather a loose confederation of regional powers, among them dynastic states, ecclesiastic republics, free cities and many small rulers owing allegiance only to the emperor in far-away Vienna, a conglomerate rather than a centralized powerhouse. The sum total of the power that the constituent princely territories, free cities, bishoprics and minor fiefdoms represented always exceeded the emperor's control. As the seventeenth-century jurist Samuel von Pufendorf put it, the Reich was *monstro simile:* it defied any classic definition of political science; neither Roman nor Holy nor an Empire, it was said. But the tradition of the empire was a powerful spiritual and cultural cement, and it also served the interests of the individual German rulers as much as those of the foreign powers. The French king, Cardinal Richelieu, could more easily part with a fat province than the freedom of the German princes to form alliances with foreign powers against the emperor in Vienna. The ancient Reich, while it lasted, was unable to organize attack, but was strong in defense. It kept old bonds of loyalty, oversaw the coinage and constituted a system of equilibrium within the emerging European balance of power.

For most Germans, history, as far as memory would take them, was a horrendous sequence of disasters in which the German lands had seemed to play the role of chessboard in peace and battlefield in war. In recent memory, there had never been a period to which Germans could look back as their "Golden Eeuw," like the Dutch, or their "Grand Siècle," like the French. The unspeakable horrors of the Thirty Years War remained part of the common heritage of the Germans, in terms like the "Swedish drink"—referring to a horrible torture used to make people talk. When peace finally came in 1648, two out of three inhabitants of the German lands were dead, victims of robbers and soldiers—professions that had often merged into each other—of hunger and the plague. The country was a desert, villages had been razed, the wealth of the great cities squandered, the pride of the burghers broken for generations to come: a deep melancholy pervaded a land shrouded in angst. From this came not only the Hobbesian notion of the strong state, but also the deep spirituality audible in the music of Dietrich Buxtehude from Lübeck, Georg Philipp Telemann from Hamburg and that towering figure Johann Sebastian Bach from Leipzig. After 1700 the War of the Spanish Succession added more scars to Germany, most of them less romantic than the ruined palace of Heidelberg, blown up by the retreating French. In the mid-eighteenth century, war came back to Germany. What the Spanish, French and British experienced as naval and colonial warfare for the control of India, the Caribbean and Canada—the Austrian Succession Wars 1740–8 and the Seven Years War 1756–63—were remembered by the Germans as houses in flame, the currency turned into dirty copper, hunger, bankruptcy and no work, young men herded into armies before they were left to die on the battlefields between the Rhine and the Oder.

Long before those scars could heal or, as the German saying goes, grass could grow over the graves, the French Revolution and the Napoleonic Wars brought more disasters. Since 1793 French armies had swept across the whole of western Europe, redrawing the map of Germany. In 1804 the Holy Roman Empire simply ceased to exist when Francis II in Vienna laid down a crown that had become, over the last hundred years, nothing but a piece of precious metal, with magic no longer radiating from it. In the same year the "Premier Consul" in Paris, Napoleon Bonaparte, crowned himself "Empereur des Français": among his "Français" not only many Germans, Italians and Dutch, but also, as obedient and grateful allies in the Confederation of the Rhine, most of the German princes.

In 1806 the Prussian government, isolated and ill advised, collected what little courage it had, ended its neutrality, declared war on Napoleon and was duly defeated at Jena. However, what was left of Prussia, half its former size, gained new strength through a revolution from above infused with the spirit of German idealism. Reformist civil servants like Baron von Stein, Wilhelm von Humboldt (brother of Alexander the explorer) and Count Hardenberg proclaimed that what the state had lost in material strength it had to replace through intellectual effort and moral energy. At much the same time, military reformers, led by intellectual generals like Scharnhorst and Gneisenau, studied French military achievements, incorporated the basic tenets of Carnot's revolutionary army and created a modern Prussian one, based on patriotism, merit and general conscription. The Jews were emancipated, and a slow and painful assimilation began. The centuries-old guild system was suppressed, following the Enlightenment conception that every man had the right to pursue happiness, even if he never caught it. The feudal system was abolished and peasants, no longer bound to the land, were turned into farmers owning the land. The land-owning nobility still tried to keep up appearances, but they were overtaken materially by untitled rural entrepreneurs, who knew how to reap a golden harvest at a time of expanding population.

Sebastian Haffner, an émigré journalist from Germany and later a great and influential historian in post-war Germany, summed up the two most decisive conclusions that the Germans had drawn from the French Revolution and Napoleon: "This shall never happen to us again!" and "We can do better!" Throughout Europe the reaction to Napoleon's conquest was to be the rise of modern nationalism as a means to reconstitute society and to give expression to popular forces. Democracy and the modern nation-state were born together; first in North America, then in France and Germany.

For the hundred years before Bismarck's revolution from above, there were two organizing principles at work in the German lands: one steeped in tradition, of the individual states, cities or principalities; the other coming in on the wings of the Enlightenment, seeking equality and with it the great promise of a better life, of a richer future, of self-fulfillment. This latter idea was especially potent to those Germans who were alienated, young and wanted to change, if not the world, then certainly Germany. Both the French Revolution and the "wars of liberation," as the uprising against Napoleon was called, gave a boost to revolutionary idealism.

After the eventual defeat of Napoleon's armies, the Congress of Vienna confirmed the fundamental simplification of the map of central Europe: it restored Prussia, but with disconnected western provinces; created a new equilibrium, with France being admitted as one of the five dominant powers; and installed the "Holy Alliance" of Russia, Austria and Prussia to forestall territorial or political change in central Europe. What came to be called the *System Metternich,* named after Austria's powerful Chancellor, Prince Metternich, was meant to be a fortress protecting the status quo.

"Deutschland Deutschland über alles"—there are few pieces of political poetry as ill understood by Germans and non-Germans alike as the revolutionary lines that a young firebrand by the name of Hoffmann von Fallersleben put on paper, denouncing the suppression exercised by the *System Metternich.* What young Hoffmann meant was pure German idealism: the idea that Germany, an open and just society lubricated by Riesling, full of song and beautiful German womanhood, should reign supreme over the 38 or so sovereignties loosely united in the German Confederation—the system constructed by the Congress of Vienna to keep the German territories neatly divided so that Europe remained in balance. It was a forward-looking song sung to the melody, ironically, of an Austrian hymn dedicated to the Emperor by Joseph Haydn, and it was incompatible with Germany's surviving *ancien régime*.

With the defeat of Napoleon and the end of his continental system of economic warfare against Britain, the nascent industries of Prussia had suddenly been exposed to the cruel impact of superior British producers. While in political terms the Prussian administration wanted to preserve the past and continue on the path of enlightened absolutism, in economic terms the Berlin authorities opened the floodgates of the market economy because they were in need of British goodwill, capital and technology. Population pressure demanded that the State encourage employment, otherwise Prussia's rulers would follow where France's *ancien régime* had led. In 1828 Prussia and Hesse concluded a customs union, built on a common market with low tariffs for the outside world, especially British industries. Six years later this was followed by the Zollverein, comprising all of northern Germany with the sole exception of the Hanseatic cities, such as Lübeck, Hamburg and Bremen. Prussia's liberal bureaucrats, most of them former students of the philosopher Immanuel Kant in Königsberg, had scored a triple victory. They had put the Prussian monarchy on the road to economic liberalism, hoping that one day political liberalism would follow. They had ended the predominance of Austria and saw it as only a matter of time before the south German states joined too. And they had, in economic terms, forged an alliance with Britain.

This happy state of affairs was cruelly tested in the 1840s. Poor harvests, which drove the price of bread sky high, coincided with a destructive industrial crisis. This was Karl Marx's defining moment and inspired him and his co-author Friedrich Engels to publish the *Communist Manifesto* in February 1848. Mass unemployment, soaring interest rates and the collapse of many companies and banks resulted in turmoil and upheaval. Open revolt began on the streets of Paris and was followed by the flight of King Louis Philippe. The exciting news spread immediately via telegraph, unleashing the revolutions of 1848 and 1849 throughout Germany and the Austrian Empire. For some months, the monarchies of central Europe looked as fragile as a house of cards.

This was Bismarck's moment, although he would have been an outstanding man at most moments in any age. The prose of his letters was akin to the best German written by Heinrich Heine and Thomas Mann; his parliamentary speeches, although delivered in a high-pitched voice, were as rich in metaphor as in substance; his diplomatic dispatches later had the rare quality of combining an overall picture of often difficult situations with clear directives as to what action to take. He was full of ambition and ambiguity, of energy but also of frustration. He had shortened his military service as best he could, but then found life as a higher civil servant humiliating and boring. After having retired to his family's run-down estates, he confessed to a cousin, "I want to make music in my own way, or not at all." His ambition, he continued, was "directed more at avoiding having to obey than to giving orders." He talked about patriotism and how it had led a few famous statesmen to their destiny. But what would lead him was something else: "ambition, the wish to command, to be admired and celebrated."

Politics was not Bismarck's passion unless, he confessed, he could be Caesar or Cromwell. In 1847 he was sent, as a replacement for a deceased deputy, into Prussia's United Landtag, whose chief task it was to vote the credits for the railway linking Berlin to the eastern provinces—a strategic more than a commercial proposition. The vast majority of the parliamentarians wanted the railway and were ready to vote the credits, but only on condition that the government honored its age-old promise to grant a constitution. Bismarck rose to the occasion and proved himself a staunch supporter of the old regime. "I am a Junker," the country gentleman farming his own land was heard to say, and he wanted to stay in that God-given position. The French Revolution overshadowed his age, and he was against it. One year later, when the streets of Berlin had seen riots, soldiers shooting, the King expressing his regrets and the troops withdrawing, Bismarck wanted to persuade the generals to stage a coup. But the young hothead was alone. So instead he became co-founder of the Conservative Party and a newspaper, proving that he understood the rules of the political mass market. Moreover, he gained a sinister reputation: "Only to be used when bayonets are fixed," King Frederick William IV noted of his unruly subject.

The year 1848 was a defining one for Bismarck, when he learned who was friend and who was foe. His time came when the revolution was over, or almost so. The Prussian government, after dithering throughout the revolutionary months about taking up the cause of German nationalism, finally decided to form a North German Union. But Russia and Austria mobilized armies, and the government in

Berlin decided that moderation was the better part of valor. In the Prussian parliament, tempers were hot; the liberals were ready to go to war, while the conservatives were for peace and the status quo with Austria. Bismarck saved the day for His Majesty's government, talking, with utter contempt, about the "national swindle" and that it was unworthy of a great power, such as Prussia, to go to war over anything but its own manifest interest. This sounded reassuring, and in due course Bismarck became Prussia's chief diplomat at the Bundestag in Frankfurt, meeting under Austrian presidency. But it was here that the Prussian diehard turned into the man of *Realpolitik*—a key term of the times. Bismarck understood two important things: that Austria was too old to survive and that it was up to Prussia to try and harness the great national passions of modern times, which otherwise would be left to the protagonists of 1848, the liberals and socialists, who were down but not out.

Better harvests, the injection of government silver and gold reserves into the general banking system, political frustration and foreign intervention—the Russians sent an army into Hungary, while the British navy staged a show of strength in the Baltic—all helped to overcome the revolutionary furore. The old rulers of Germany escaped catastrophe, but only by the skin of their teeth. And they had learned their lesson. They granted constitutional compromises in order to bring the moneyed classes on to their side. But the chief remedy was economic—a powerful drive towards industrialization and capitalism throughout the German lands allowed private bankers to follow the lead of the French Crédit Mobilier and to set up the joint-stock universal banks, which were to be at the heart of corporate Germany's rise and rise. Money came out of its hiding places; investors, not least from Britain, hoped for riches in the boom economy now taking off. The gold rushes in North America and Australia stoked up demand. Throughout the 1860s the north German economy registered overall annual growth of between 8 and 10 percent.

Bismarck observed the rise of Napoleon III from adventurer to prince president in 1848 and to Emperor in 1852 with fascination, and learned a useful lesson. Conservatism, if it kept the masses content with bread and circuses, was a force for the future and could muster popular support. This was a recipe that the Prussian monarchy had yet to try, but in 1862 when King William I and his parliament, dominated by liberal radicals, found themselves in full conflict over army reform and constitutional rights, the moment was ripe. The King was ready to abdicate in favor of the Crown Prince who, married to Queen Victoria's eldest daughter, was full of liberal English ideas. The military leaders sent one telegram after another trying to recall Bismarck, who had just been sent as Prussian ambassador to Paris. But the recipient pretended ignorance. Instead, he was busy persuading his wife that the ambassador's residence, a palatial building in the rue de Lille overlooking the Seine, was too modest for her, and that he was not ready for her arrival. The truth was that he had developed an infatuation with Countess Katharina Orloff, wife of the Russian ambassador. However, eventually, opting for ambition over love, Bismarck did travel to Potsdam, where he talked the King out of his somber thoughts. He promised not to stage a coup or to alienate the Austrians or surrender to parliament. When made Prime Minister, he did not fully keep any of these promises. He ran the country without a legally approved budget law, he fought a war against

Austria, overthrowing the German Confederation, and in the end he even forged an understanding with the liberals in parliament.

Having been in the Wilhelmstrasse for only a few days, Bismarck fired the opening shot of his grand strategy in the budget committee of the Prussian parliament. "It is not through speeches and majority voting that the great questions of our time are answered—that has been the great illusion of 1848–49—but through iron and blood." The liberals were duly shocked, but they also wanted national unification, if necessary through a military showdown. Bismarck understood that this was now his best chance of moving forward and starting what soon turned out to be nothing short of a revolution from above.

The Six Weeks War of 1864 against Denmark—unwisely, the Danish King had tried to incorporate his German provinces, Schleswig and Holstein, situated between the North Sea, the Baltic and Hamburg, into the Danish nation-state—was a military walkover for the combined forces of Prussia and Austria, and finally the elusive Schleswig-Holstein question that had provoked vast nationalistic passion in Germany and Denmark, a short war in 1848 and another sixteen years later, seemed to have been solved. Lord Palmerston, then British Prime Minister, dismissively remarked that there were only three people who understood what he termed the Schleswig-Holstein question: "one was the Prince Consort who is dead, another one a German scholar who has gone mad, and the third one is me, and I have forgotten."

The victory over the Danish army was nothing but a primer for much larger diplomatic and military operations. In fact, Bismarck ensured that harmony between Vienna and Berlin, the victors of the war in 1866, was not to last. While keeping the pressure on the liberals in Berlin, he started a sweeping campaign for an all-German parliament. This was impossible for the Austrians to accept, since direct elections throughout the far-flung and diverse possessions of the Habsburg Empire would have been the beginning of the end for that fragile construct held together by nothing but the Emperor, the Catholic Church, the aristocracy and the largely German-speaking civil service. In the spring of 1866, Bismarck concluded a military alliance with Italy, limited to three months, to put more pressure on the Austrians. In addition, he let the Prussian bankers clean out the European capital markets. When war came, Austria had as allies the Kingdom of Hanover, the Electorate of Hesse and the entire south, including the Free City of Frankfurt. In retrospect, the war seems to have had more of the formal quality of a duel, with the final exchange of shots at Königgrätz. While the King and his generals wanted to ride triumphantly into Vienna, Bismarck would have nothing of the kind. He foresaw that he would one day need Austria as an ally, and he wanted no cheap triumphs at the expense of a pillar of the *ancien régime*. He insisted, however, that Hesse and Hanover were taken off the map of Europe and turned into Prussian provinces. Frankfurt and Nassau suffered the same fate.

Germany after 1866 was in all but name the Germany of 1871. The Prussian parliament accepted defeat, and Bismarck was generous enough to allow the liberals to forgive him his extraconstitutional excursion. The north was united in a confederation, with a common constitution under Prussian presidency. The south—Bavaria, Baden, Hesse, Württemberg—was integrated through the Customs Union, now with a law-making parliament instead of a mere diplomatic assemblage. The military alliances that put the south German troops on the same footing as the Prussians were of equal importance. The result was an extended Prussian army, which as Bismarck could sense might well be needed in the not too distant future against the France of Napoleon III.

The Franco-Prussian War of 1870 was short and swift, at least in its first phase against the imperial armies of Napoleon III, before the French republican authorities conducted their war *à l'outrance*, to the death, but also ending in defeat. In his opening move, Field Marshal von Moltke had delivered a masterpiece of strategy, using the railways to encircle the French armies at Sedan and, after a few weeks, forcing the French Emperor into an armistice. Meanwhile, the bloody battles in Alsace and Lorraine, where Bavarian and other troops were engaged, made German patriotism surge and gave the Bismarckian construction that magic blessing that only war or revolution, or both, can bestow, fusing the German states into a single entity under the control of Prussia or, more precisely, Bismarck and the Berlin administration.

Altogether, the political and social revolutions of 1848 and the industrial revolution had challenged the old established order of state and society. The shockwaves of the French Revolution and Napoleon could still be felt throughout the German lands, and they carried with them many promises and many threats. Bismarck's was a revolution from above to exorcise and paralyze the ghosts of 1789 and 1848. But it was still a revolution albeit in the guise of the old order. Bismarck's achievement was to have put a stop to the looming social and political changes in Germany. But, by implication, this entailed a transformation of the European system as well. This was what Benjamin Disraeli had in mind when warning Her Majesty's government in 1871 against the wider implications of what he termed the "German revolution."

2

THE BISMARCK YEARS

The industrial revolution in Germany meant that wages rose for the vast majority of the population, beginning in the 1850s. Men and women alike had a chance of living longer and happier lives, and they had a justified expectation that one day their children would fare even better. But what mattered most to the Germans of Bismarck's day was the hope that the era of angst was a thing of the past. Certainly the prevailing mood was one of confidence and optimism, in spite of the many casualties of industrial progress and capitalist transformation and the ensuing resentment, fear of the future and social upheaval. After the Great War, people would refer to the Bismarckian and Wilhelmine past as the good old days—*die gute alte Zeit*—and they grieved for the years when peace and progress seemed the norm.

There were various political persuasions within the new Germany after that cold and colorful January day at Versailles, 1871. Enthusiasm for the new turn of events among the liberals was great, almost unlimited, provided that through the Reichstag they could persuade Bismarck to go along with free trade and nation building. They also wished to curb the influence of both major churches and ensure minimal liaison with labor leaders. Unfortunately, the liberals were deeply split. The left wing was composed of 1848ers from Württemberg and the old provinces of Prussia, who had led the charge against royal prerogative. They had tried to squeeze more parliamentary powers out of King William I when he wanted army reform, and they had been the bedrock of opposition against Bismarck ever since 1862 when he assumed office. These liberals saw the constitutional compromise of 1867, when the north German Reichstag had settled scores with Bismarck, merely as a starting point for many more rounds of constitutional wrangling.

Moving distinctly to the right, the National Liberals were by and large a new party. They enthusiastically endorsed the Prussian annexation of the Kingdom of Hanover and the Electorate of Hesse, of Hesse-Nassau and of the Free City of Frankfurt after 1866. They were happy with the Prussian concept of a free-trade oriented economic area, already embodied in the German customs union, with legislation and jurisdiction about to be united throughout Germany together with one currency and one central bank. For the National Liberal leaders and their flock, 1848 was a closed chapter, best forgotten.

However, the conservatives were far from triumphant. They had misgivings about Bismarck's Caesarism, his courting of public opinion, his warmongering against Austria, which was adding oil to the flames of modern nationalism, and his severing of links between throne and altar by taking up the fight for the secular state. To them, the Bismarckian answer to the revolutionary sea change of 1848 had a mephistophelean smell, his alliance with modern nationalism to them was as good as a pact with the Devil. It was only in the course of the 1870s, when the great Prussian agricultural estates east of the Elbe began to suffer under the unforgiving impact of world markets, that the bargain between Prussian conservatives and Bismarck's regime was put on a new, largely economic footing. Neither could afford to do without the other in the common battle against socialists, liberals, the world market and free trade.

A key part of the political spectrum in Bismarck's Germany was the German Center Party, a kind of action committee of political Catholicism. "Il mondo casca" was the cry in the Vatican when, in 1866, the forces of Catholic Austria and their German allies were defeated by the Prussians, who in turn were allied with the Italy of Cavour and Vittorio Emmanuele—arch opponents of the secular power of the Pope. In fact it had been clear ever since 1848 that the clergy, Protestant and Catholic alike, would sooner or later have to be forced to retire into the churches and the universities and lose control of education and charity, except on the margins of society. Throughout German Catholicism, concentrated in the Rhineland, in Silesia and in Bavaria, the battle cry was to unite and set up a political party, to build a bastion against the onslaught of secularism. The Center Party was referred to by its adherents as the *Zentrums-Turm,* the tower. Because of its organizing principle in the Catholic religion, it was the only political party to unite a cross-section of the population, from laborer to aristocrat, from industrialist to bishop. It did not increase the Center Party's popularity among national minded liberals that, in the name of Catholicism, the Poles from Prussia's eastern provinces and the French from the newly acquired *Reichslande,* Alsace and Lorraine, joined the parliamentary party. The Center Party cut across class barriers and transcended the nation-state. The label "Ultramontane," soon applied to it, was not meant to flatter. It insinuated that its leaders received their guidelines from beyond the Alps—*ultra montes*—that is, from the Vatican. In fact, when one of the first parliamentary initiatives of the Center Party in 1871 was to call upon the German Reich to send troops to Italy and protect the Pope against the secular Italian state, Bismarck found his worst suspicions of a Europe-wide Catholic conspiracy corroborated. For the next few years, the Catholics were denounced, just as much as the socialists, as *Reichsfeinde*, enemies of the empire.

The *Kulturkampf*, nominally Bismarck's attack on Catholicism, was directed not so much against religion as against the secular power of both major churches and the meddling of priests and pastors in affairs not their own. It had started in the Rhineland, where the Catholic Church was the mainstay of opposition to the Prussian-Protestant predominance. But the government of Bavaria added oil to the flames by demanding that there should be a formal ban on politicizing by priests, that civil matters like marriage and divorce should be taken out of the hands of the churches, and that monastic orders which did not comply should be evicted. Bismarck immediately seized the chance to divide and rule.

Concomitantly, he was also hostile towards the old-style conservatives in rural Prussia east of Berlin. In their orthodoxy and pietism, they opposed him as well as his *nouveau riche* Reich and his alliance with liberalism and secularism, so threatening to undermine his sway over King William I. The *Kulturkampf*, largely through Reich and *Land* legislation, drew the line between Church and State as in France, and it lasted for the best part of a decade. Thereafter the Center Party was needed in parliament to secure a majority loyal to Bismarck. But neither side could ever be sure of the other. Bismarck wanted, if he could have it, the combined support of conservatives and liberals, and to manage without the Catholic party; the Center Party, in its turn, could ill afford to alienate its working-class wing. Moreover, the party leaders would take as their lodestar the Papal encyclicals, especially *Rerum Novarum* in 1890, when the Pope gave an answer to the social question that was impossible to reconcile with free-wheeling capitalism. The Center Party was neither democratic nor anti-democratic; it was more conservative than liberal, but it was also more left wing than right wing. In short, it was the party of Catholicism.

The Social Democratic Party was even more of a misfit in the German political spectrum. After his untimely death in a duel for the honor of Countess Hatzfeld, Ferdinand Lassalle left the socialist field to the small entrepreneur August Bebel, a woodturner who made himself the most redoubtable socialist leader. His followers proudly referred to him as the *Arbeiter Bismarck,* "the workers' Bismarck." Bebel studied Marx's writings while in prison during the Franco-German war, but he was too practical a man to follow them literally. Bismarck's summary dismissal of him and his socialist followers as *Reichsfeinde*—enemies of the empire—somehow missed the point that Bebel and his colleagues, of whom there were a mere handful in the Reichstag of 1871, did not oppose national unification as such. What they wanted was a different kind of Germany, not Bismarck's authoritarianism, not pure capitalism, but a market economy with a strong state and a lot of social warmth to it.

Bebel could never be accused of being over-pragmatic: he praised the Paris Commune of 1871, in spite of its bloody excesses, as the vanguard of the European proletariat and the model to which German workers aspired. Fortunately, however, Bebel did not press that point and when two assassination attempts were made on the old Emperor in 1878 and 1879, and in both cases the culprits confessed to some sympathy for the socialist cause, it was Bebel who preached the sermon of evolution and the belief in the metaphorical "wheel of history." He thus put clear ground between the German socialists and the practices of anarchism and revolutionary terror such as were displayed in Russia and elsewhere. Most German social democrats were in fact petit bourgeois and pragmatic, wearing black suits and bowler hats when demonstrating. They carried with them the legacy of many centuries of guild life: journeymen had always aspired to becoming part of good society and now they were moving closer to that promised land.

The social democrats were not suppressed, let alone persecuted, by the anti-socialist law of 1879 that was introduced as an answer to the assaults on the Kaiser—and also to help Bismarck form a new, pro-government majority. It permitted them to function in the Reichstag, but not to engage in public campaigning. Twelve years later the socialists had risen to more than 25 percent of the popular vote in industrial centers, while the liberals had lost support and declined in numbers and influence. This showed the futility of Bismarck's somewhat half-hearted anti-socialist law and, when he fell, this piece of legislation went too, never to be revived.

The German political system combined elements of both royal absolutism and parliamentary democracy in an uneasy compromise. In its day it was referred to as "German constitutionalism" and was more often than not justified on the grounds of the exposed geostrategic situation of the country in the middle of Europe. There was no *Reichsregierung,* as Bismarck once pointedly observed. There was only the Reichskanzler taking political responsibility: the Chancellor with his office of a few higher civil servants. Bismarck had seen to it when the constitution was set up that it remained open from whom this responsibility was derived: from the monarch, most likely; from history, most certainly; from the Reichstag let alone the electorate, most certainly not. There were, of course, a number of state secretaries: one for the treasury, one for foreign affairs, one for naval matters, another one for postal services, one for home affairs, one for questions of jurisdiction. But a state secretary answerable to the Reichstag for the largest chunk of the budget, military expenditure, was conspicuous in his absence. The military budget had to be administered through the Prussian Ministry of War, while all matters concerning the royal—not imperial—*Kommandogewalt*, the military backbone of the State, rested with the monarch, who, claiming royal prerogative, would handle all matters of military advancement and deployment through the Militärkabinett.

State secretaries could not be members of the Reichstag and that meant that this body had no interlocutor except Bismarck. All important administrative work was done by the Prussian administration and overseen by the Staatsministerium of Prussia, the Prussian cabinet. Prussian ministers were also superior in rank to mere state secretaries of the Reich. Within this construction not only the Reichstag had little influence; even the individual states could not exercise any significant measure of control. It also implied that military absolutism remained almost undiluted except for the army budget, and that was voted not annually, but for many years in advance. As long as Bismarck kept his influence over the King of Prussia and German Emperor, the Iron Chancellor was, in all but name, the ruler of Germany.

However, the German Reichstag, although far from powerless, could not vote a government out of office. Without finding or manufacturing a majority, the government would have found it impossible to function. But, in competition with parliament and political parties, there developed a vast array of organized interests, pressure groups and media claiming a role in that open-ended opera called the German polity. This opera may have been democratic in parts, especially when it came to one-man, one-vote elections. But above all it was functional, translating ever more diverse and indeed controversial interests into a political process as unpredictable as the purest of democracies.

The Iron Chancellor did everything to overcome the consequences of what he, the white revolutionary, had achieved. His domestic policy was carefully crafted to preserve a social balance in which the landed interest was paramount. But this was a losing battle against the growing strength of industry, vital in any case to provide jobs for the rapidly increasing population. The laws curtailing the rights of the social democrats, passed in 1878, had to be compensated for by the introduction, far ahead of other countries, of state insurance against the effects of old age, sickness and accidents, starting in 1883 and soon turning into a massive system of self-administration overseen by the State. Bismarck's attack on Catholics had to be broken off in order to win their vote. Colonial propaganda was drummed up, but failed to rouse much public enthusiasm. Domestic politics were overshadowed by the great depression of the 1870s and 1880s and the resulting battles between protectionists and free traders: the former, the landed interest and heavy industry; the latter, the export-oriented manufacturers of machine tools and the like, the socialists and the left wing of the liberals.

In foreign policy Bismarck preached, time and again, the blessings of peace, equilibrium and the status quo. He had been converted by *le cauchemar des coalitions*—the nightmare of coalitions—to the lost wisdom of the Congress of

Vienna, back in 1815. The Austro-Hungarian Emperor Franz-Joseph needed tranquility to keep his multinational empire together. The Tsar needed tranquility to prevent the resurrection of Poland—divided between Russia, Austria and Prussia at the end of the eighteenth century. Bismarck cultivated alliances with both Russia and Austria, but due to the stirrings of the Balkan Slavs against their Turkish overlords, this became increasingly difficult, and the much trumpeted Three Emperors' Alliance of the early years threatened to end in war. There was a strong Pan-Slav movement within Russia, which demanded that the Tsar intervene on behalf of their Balkan cousins, more especially the Serbs. But any increase in Balkan nationalism or interference by other states in the region was highly dangerous for the Austrian Empire. Bismarck had given assurances to the Russians, saying that the whole of the Balkans was "not worth the healthy bones of a Pomeranian musketeer." However, this did not prevent a confrontation between Austria and Russia, caused by the latter's war with Turkey. Consequently, Bismarck had to call a European congress at Berlin in the summer of 1878. In doing so, he saved the face of Austria for the time being and probably prevented a major war between the British Empire and Russia over who would control the eastern Mediterranean. Bismarck claimed to have acted merely as an "honest broker"—his banker, Gerson von Bleichröder, commented that there is no such thing. At any rate, the Russians were ungrateful and disappointed, the Pan-Slavist press began to agitate against Germany, and the Tsar wrote an angry letter to his uncle, the German Emperor, complaining about Bismarck and his support for Britain and Austria.

In 1879 the German Reichstag retaliated against a doubling of Russian import duties—the Russians suddenly insisted on payment in gold instead of half-price paper rubles—by introducing protective tariffs for German agriculture, and this economic pressure enhanced the alienation. Only one year after his diplomatic triumph at the Congress of Berlin, Bismarck again tried to mend diplomatic fences, concluding a dual alliance with Austria and then, for balance, a new alliance with Russia. But the latter had to remain a secret because public opinion in both countries would have been opposed to it. In 1887, in the face of much warlike talk, a secret "Reinsurance Treaty" was added, amid growing hostility between Austria and Russia over the Balkans. The treaty, to last for three years, specified that in case of war both Russia and Germany were to observe neutrality: Germany in the case of a war between Russia and Austria, Russia in the case of war with France. Nobody thought that the Reinsurance Treaty was worth very much. But it was to give Germany breathing space if war broke out, and it was also meant to have a sobering effect on Vienna and St. Petersburg, as neither could count on automatic German support.

Bismarck insisted that Germany was, by now, solely interested in maintaining the status quo, saying, "We are what old Prince Metternich called a saturated power." In reality, Bismarck found himself in the role of the sorcerer's apprentice, who had lost the words of the spell to get the genie back in the bottle. There had been too much upheaval, too much social change, and there had been the industrial revolution.

Germany's industrial revolution had begun on the Lower Rhine and in the Ruhr area during the final decades of the eighteenth century, then in Berlin and Silesia, while the centuries-old industrial centers south of the Main river lagged behind for want of capital, technology, access to markets and, not least, coal to fire the furnaces. In the long run, this would prove to be a blessing in disguise, as southerners had to cultivate their ancient metallurgical skills and apply them to modern machinery. Such was the case of Gottlieb Daimler and Karl Benz in Stuttgart and Mannheim respectively, working on the motor car, or of Robert Bosch who, after a long apprenticeship on the east coast of the United States, supplied the electrical equipment required by the car. But nineteenth-century industrial Germany was built on coal and steel and textiles, on railways and canals, and most of these were to be found in the crescent of prosperity stretching from Aachen in the west via Cologne and Essen to Berlin, and from Berlin to the coal mines and mills of Upper Silesia.

Bismarck's revolution from above had coincided with the building of a powerhouse at the heart of the continent. Once most of the main lines were completed, machine tools took over from railways as the leading sector, getting a second wind when, even before the turn of the century, electricity was harnessed to production. A vast building boom gave employment to small-scale manufacturers of household appliances and encouraged many old-style artisans to try their hand in larger undertakings. The textile industry of Krefeld expanded, as did that of northern Bavaria and around Plauen in Saxony. The chemical industry, in the past concentrating almost entirely on raw materials, now found vast markets for fertilizers, pharmaceuticals and artificial dyes. In the 1860s almost overnight Badische Anilin- und Soda-Fabrik (BASF) turned the fishing village of Ludwigshafen, at the confluence of the Neckar and the Rhine, into an industrial landscape of

giant proportions. The same was true of Meister Lucius &
Brüning in Hoechst on the Main, and of the Bayer works,
best known for aspirin, in Leverkusen on the Rhine.

Germany's industrial revolution had started on the
principle of free trade and this remained the keynote well
into the 1870s. But then the business climate changed
throughout the Atlantic world. In May 1873 the Vienna
stock exchange collapsed, then Berlin's and Frankfurt's followed suit. For the past fifteen years or so, stocks had been
rising with new companies springing up left and right,
bringing fortunes to investors, banks and speculators—
Gründungsfieber, "founding mania," as the conservative Cas-
sandras called it, had become a contagious disease. But
now the tide turned inexorably, and no longer could the
liberals hope that it would carry them to power. Conservative fundamentalism came into its own, seeing the old
Prussia, with its Protestant value system and its rigid social
hierarchy, going to ruin. Frustration with the capitalist
wealth machine that had suddenly come to a halt gave rise
to anti-Semitism, the losers finding the root of all evil in
the lust for money and the stock exchange; seeing the new
Reich as some giant, godless casino.

To add to the dark mood of pessimism, German heavy
industry began to suffer from British and Belgian competition. The reaction was twofold: pressure on the government to revise trade policy and protect "national work,"
and the formation of special interest groups to change the
mood in the Reichstag, the media and the population at
large. The National Liberals proved to be most attentive to
the lamentations—and the money—of the barons of heavy
industry, while the Fortschrittspartei, the left wing of the
liberal movement, represented more the export-oriented

machine-tool industry, which saw protectionism as a threat to its booming business with the rest of the world.

An even more serious blow to the social and political equilibrium came from Russia and the United States, which were exporting increasing tonnages of cheap wheat and rye to Germany. The vast prairies of the Midwest, recently connected by railroad to the seaports, especially Baltimore, could produce at very low cost and then ship the grain at cheap rates thanks to the impact of steamers. The landowners and farmers on the north German plains soon became desperate and brought pressure to bear on the Conservative Party and on the government. They received a sympathetic hearing from Bismarck, whose agricultural instincts had easily survived all the free-trade lessons that his banker Gerson Bleichröder might have administered. He immediately understood that here was the material to forge a solid and docile center-right coalition of *Rittergut und Hochofen,* the landed estate and the blast furnace.

In 1879 the first protectionist tariff had been passed in the Reichstag, helped by vast unrest over the suspected implication of the social democrats in the two recent attempts on the old Kaiser's life. For Bismarck the new tariff was welcome not only as a means of transforming the Reichstag and securing a loyal majority, but also as a way to increase the revenue of the Reich administration, until then often dependent on transfers from the individual states, especially Prussia. In this, however, he scored only half a victory. The states, led by the Prussian administration, were strong enough to ensure that the money collected at the customs offices went to them first, and only then, if they so wished, to the Reich.

For decades, protectionism versus free trade continued to be the defining issue in the German parliament and in public debate. In 1887 another round of tariffs was added to save the landowners from bankruptcy and the Bismarckian coalition from falling apart. But the cost was high, not only to German industry and the ever-growing number of urban consumers, but also in terms of foreign policy. Tsarist Russia, forever dependent on the German banks to finance its industrialization and infrastructure, was hard hit by the customs duties thrown on the sole product that it could export—wheat from the Ukraine. Close to 30 percent of Russia's imports came from Germany and close to 30 percent of its exports went to Germany. In 1876 the Russian government had imposed double import duties on German machinery and rail equipment, causing an outcry among industry, to which Bismarck was quick to respond. Through the 1880s the language became increasingly threatening, while Bismarck, for internal reasons, found it impossible to give way and grant the Russians the trade treaty and the low tariffs that they kept demanding. He must have known, better than anybody else, that he was putting at risk the vital alliance with Germany's awesome eastern neighbor. In 1887, at the time of the reinsurance treaty, Bismarck threw the gauntlet down before the Russians by letting it be known to the board of the Berlin stock exchange that it would be unwise in the future to accept Russian bonds as first-rate securities. This was not only insulting, but also meant higher interest rates for the Russians—and so it gave support to the Franco-Russian alliance that was already in the making.

After more than two decades at the helm of Prussia and Germany, Bismarck's regime began to unravel. In foreign policy his system of alliances showed serious strain: France could no longer be marginalized now that the Paris–St. Petersburg alliance was in the making. On the domestic scene his anti-socialist legislation had not delivered final victory over the enemy, and even his forward looking social legislation had not been effective in curbing the rise of socialism throughout industrial Germany. Both the Catholic center party and the two liberal parties began to question the wisdom and the leadership of the old man in the Wilhelmstrasse. The Emperor with his unquestioning loyalty to Bismarck would not live forever—a change of government was in the offing. Bismarck had become, long before he fell from power, a monument to his own past.

3

MANY GERMANYS

The new Germany of 1871 was deeply ambiguous about its untried European role, and so were the Germans regarding their new identity. Most of the 41 million people living within the German borders, now including France's lost daughters Alsace and Lorraine, would have described themselves not as Germans but, full of proud regionalism and local patriotism, as Bavarians, Prussians, Badeners, Saxons, etc. In the ports of the North Sea and the Baltic, people would identify themselves as *Hanseaten,* referring to the medieval glories of the Hanse, a powerful merchant alliance commanding the waves and the commerce carried on them. These self-descriptions always had an undertone, and still have, setting those using them apart from the German nation at large, from Bismarck and Berlin. But even Bismarck and the Emperor whom he created would, if asked, have readily described themselves as Prussians or, even further back in the mists of history, as Brandenburgers. Bismarck at times would call himself a "kurbrandenburgischer Vasall" of the Prussian King; at times he would insist on the fact that his forefathers had held landed estates in the Altmark long before the Hohenzollern dynasty arrived, from Nuremberg, in 1416.

German federalism was, and still is, the most tangible constitutional expression of this perennial desire of Germans to distance themselves from the center, from Bonn or Berlin, from being German. One of the long-lasting complaints against the Bismarckian construction was that it was a hegemony, thinly disguised by constitutional language referring to the "alliance of the German princes and Free Cities." Prussia was dominant in economic, industrial, financial, administrative and military terms—in fact, two-thirds of the German territory was under the Prussian eagle, and three-fifths of the German population. It was also through the various Prussian ministries in the Wilhelmstrasse that the Reich "offices"—the *Reichsämter*—were run, legislation was prepared and politics was decided. The state secretaries at the helm of the *Reichsämter* clearly ranked below the Prussian ministers "with the title Excellency," as the official description went.

But even before Bavaria, Württemberg or Baden were absorbed into Bismarckian Germany—all of them put on the map by Napoleon to suit his strategic priorities—the people thus forcefully incorporated had not forgotten that their grandfathers could run their own affairs, issue their own money, decide their own taxes and had nobody above the city government or the local abbey but the faraway Holy Roman Emperor. The people of Cologne still resented the Prussian occupation that began in 1813, when the French retreated, and ended only in the mid-twentieth century. They poked fun at the Prussian heroes during their annual carnival celebrations. In 1848 the revolution there had a distinct anti-Prussian tone, and again after 1918 there was a strong wave of Rhenish separatism, away from Prussia and Berlin. In the west, where French law had been introduced, the Code Napoléon prevailed until 1900, as did the Allgemeines Landrecht für die Preussischen Staaten in the east—a much older, Enlightenment-inspired, pre-revolutionary concept of civil law.

This German diversity was deeply rooted in daily life, in bread and beer, in costume, language and local law. People spoke their local vernacular, except the classes of *Besitz und Bildung,* wealth and education, who used high German among themselves, but had to resort to local usage when talking to their servants, or to lowly neighbors. Bismarck, a writer of poetic letters and a great performer on the parliamentary rostrum, talked *Plattdeutsch* to his peasants on the Elbe, a language that no one would understand in the south. The people of Straubing on the Danube in Lower Bavaria would have felt on a different continent if they had ever traveled to Schleswig-Holstein in the north—for which, of course, they saw no need. German had many different melodies and incompatible idioms, mutually regarded as either funny or incomprehensible, or both. The people of Saxony, being blessed with a dialect at best funny, at worst offensive, were only saved through their awe-inspiring intellectual and industrial achievements.

But language was only one expression of diversity. The way houses were built or villages were laid out was vastly different throughout the country, often reflecting ancient forms of agriculture or feudal holdings. Some parts of eastern Germany, thinly populated anyway, were constantly losing people to the big cities, most notably Berlin. In the south, in Württemberg, for many centuries weaving and metal trades had allowed people a modest living in small cities, which were now almost invariably turning into thriving industrial centers.

Food, of course, added to the diversity, especially beer, as it could not be stored or transported and so had to be consumed locally. Bread and cake in curious forms often referred to historical or magic origins. The classical German bread roll came in a form that resembled the female genitals, leaving no doubt that it symbolized fertility. Bread was mostly of the dark, crusty variety, wheat being so expensive that even for the middle classes white bread was a luxury. The same was true for meat: only on Sundays. Fish was the cheap staple in the north; so cheap, indeed, that servants in Cologne, when the Rhine was still a green-and-white river revealing its alpine origins, complained of too much salmon. In the south, such fish as carp, first reared in monastic stew ponds, was popular among the rich and the poor. Cheese was anything but a delicacy. The finer varieties could not be imported from France or Switzerland, and the local, smelly varieties were mostly for the modest tables of the lower classes.

Beer was for the masses; champagne, cognac and wine for the upper classes. The wine was mostly Riesling from the Rheinpfalz or, even more sought after, from the Rhein-gau—what the British call Hock after Hochheim. Or else there was Silvaner in the strange *Bocksbeutel* bottles from Franconia, once again referring to the magic powers of fer-tility in a ram's testicles. Or again, Riesling from the Moselle, the lower Saar and the upper Rhine valley in Baden. Wine was even produced in the Elbe valley near Dresden and on the steep and stony slopes of the Saale val-ley not far from Weimar. German champagne had to be called *Sekt* after the Treaty of Versailles, while the German answer to French cognac consisted of many local spirits: plums or cherries turned into brandy in the south, potatoes and rye turned into schnapps in the north.

Even the times when people took their meals differed. For the workers, the day began at sunrise and ended, more or less, with sunset: lighting was expensive. Working days were long, often ten or more hours a day, over fifty hours a week. By contrast, having time to sleep after sunrise and being able to wine and dine into the night were clear signs of high living. Workmen would take some bread and wurst and soup with them—canteens came much later. In contrast, the day of the well-to-do would begin with a light *Sattelfrühstück* and a ride, followed by *déjeuner*—the upper-class term for lunch—and later five o'clock tea in a hotel, with elegant music, or a visit to friends. Dinner would be late in the evening: to begin before eight o'clock would have been seen as distinctly lower-class. To negotiate six or eight courses would not be regarded as outrageous: in fact, the host's business standing would be gauged by the luxuries displayed on his table, whether the Meissen, Berlin or Nymphenburg porcelain, or the caviar and champagne, fish, venison and out-of-season fruit.

Piped water was a luxury that began to be introduced only at the turn of the century, while hot water was reserved for the well-to-do. Water closets were a sign of a higher form of living, and certainly costly. Most lavatories were smelly affairs, often shared by many and usually situated outside the house in a yard, with a heart (why a heart remains an enigma) cut out of the wooden door. Bathtubs were not unknown in the old days, but were regarded as a luxury. When the old Emperor wanted a bath, he had the tub brought into the royal palace from a nearby hotel at Unter den Linden. It was only the wholesale introduction of electricity during the last years of the nineteenth century—electrical bulbs, furnished by Emil Rathenau's AEG (Allgemeine Elektrizitäts-Gesellschaft), lit imperial Berlin as early as 1876—that made daily life a little brighter, servants more expendable, conditions healthier.

Modern technology had an egalitarian dimension. The universe of the poor and the universe of the rich began to show some overlap. The bicycle allowed speed, until then an expensive commodity, to the relatively poor, and so did the railway. There were still four different classes in a passenger train: fourth class for the poor carrying unwieldy luggage, third for the middle class of modest means, second for ladies, and first for the rich. But the King of Saxony complained about the equalizing effect of railway travel, as the king and the laborer would start, and arrive, on the same train and at the same time. Time was also a great equalizer. The railways and industry required standard time, not something to be found in the old days. This and the spread of pocket watches at reasonable prices meant that the measurement of time was no longer a privilege, but a condition of daily life.

Of course, holidays were only for the affluent, greatly facilitated by the speed and safety of the railways. From Berlin, one would take the train northwards to Heiligendamm to spend a weekend on the Baltic coast in elegant neoclassical surroundings. To the south there was the French Riviera, and in between the Swiss Alps, which lost their awesome terror and began to attract the urban middle classes. Johanna Spyri's popular story of *Heidi,* the innocent and healthy little girl from the mountains near the ancient spa of Ragaz, promised health for body and soul alike. Trains and trams enabled suburbs to spread, realizing the idea of the garden city, or even a house in the country at weekends. What Hampstead was for Londoners, Grünewald and Wannsee were for Berliners, and Ebenhausen for the rich nature-lovers in Munich.

Health became a serious preoccupation as never before, and so did sport. Again, the rich and the poor divided: the upper classes proudly displayed a little English, played golf and rode horses. Students, at least the more militant ones, learned fencing, not so much for health reasons as for honor and prestige. The occasional carefully stage-managed duel was seen as a distinction of social status and would, it was hoped, result in some carefully cultivated scars on the face which were worn like a decoration, securing promotion through the invisible but powerful old boys' network. The soccer-playing masses also took part in bicycle races and boxing, the socialists seeing to it that working-class sports were well organized within their all-encompassing system of care from the cradle to the grave.

There was no one German society in the strict sense of the word. Life on an East Prussian estate, small like that of the average *Rittergut,* or vast like the landholdings of the Dönhoffs, the Dohnas or the Lehndorffs, remained pretty much in its traditional mold. But even here the agricultural depression would be felt, from the mid-1870s on, as competition came from Ukraine's fertile black soil, from the green pastures of Argentina and from the vast prairies of the American Midwest. Berlin, by contrast, was a million-strong metropolis constantly on the move, tearing down old buildings and building new ones, linking villages through rapid transit and in turn creating new industrial centers. It housed not only the power elites of old Prussia, but also the new banks, modern mass media, organized interests and political parties. In the west, the Ruhr industries were expanding rapidly. In the south, with no coal mines and no steel mills, a different kind of industrialization was under way, traditionally based on brain power and attention to detail, on the textile industry and metallurgy. There were thus many societies, but all of them were on the move. Emigration, almost exclusively to North America, continued unabated: in fact, after the 1870 war it rose to new highs. For the next twenty years, an average of 100,000 young men and women left home and family in Germany each year to seek a better life in the New World. Most of them had relatives there, who described in glowing terms the land of unlimited opportunity after the

American Civil War was over and the Wild West had been opened. This stream of emigrants continued until the great crash of 1893 occurred in North America, when the free distribution of land by the railways ended and economic prospects at home looked brighter.

Numbers emigrating were small compared to the quantity of people migrating from east to west, from Upper and Lower Silesia and the Poznan province, West Prussia and East Prussia to Berlin and beyond. Unabated population growth on the land not only created a vast reservoir of consumption, but also supplied the workforce for industry. The number of the Kaiser's subjects grew by more than 1 percent a year, from 41 million in 1871 to no fewer than 68 million in 1913. The increase in population, steadying only during the recession years 1906–7, meant that around the turn of the century the Germans were, on average, the youngest nation in Europe, with the sole exception of Russia. France's population, by contrast, had been stagnating ever since the bloodletting of the Napoleonic Wars.

Much of the youthful energy and the spirit of enterprise in Germany, but also the lack of experience, can probably be explained by this volcanic upheaval. In the cities, families tended to be smaller due to high rents and, since the 1880s, the introduction of collective systems of old-age insurance. On the land, parents still wanted many children. But the land could not accommodate them, and wages remained a pittance compared to what industry paid in the cities. So the east-west drift was complemented by a constant movement from the land to the urban agglomerations of Berlin and of the Ruhr, around Frankfurt and Stuttgart, Munich and Nuremberg, Hamburg and Bremen. Cities would soon tear down their ancient walls and develop one ring of industrial estates and housing after another, incorporating nearby villages, linking them by public transport and encouraging industries to set up factories where the workforce was to hand. Near the expanding cities, the sons of lowly peasants, selling some meager holdings for building plots for the future suburbia, became millionaires overnight and in their turn sought lucrative investments. Population growth, rising living standards, technology and the unbridled forces of capitalism created what economic historians call self-sustained growth.

As everything and everybody was on the move, class barriers were no longer insurmountable. To the geographic migration must be added movement up and down the social ladder, but mostly up. Down went the many trades to do with horses and road haulage, which were overtaken by the railway. Many shoemakers and tailors fell by the wayside when modern manufacturers took over and the sewing machine replaced the work of many artisans. In today's Germany, Schneider, Schuhmacher, Müller and Schmidt are the commonest of surnames, testifying to the strength of such trades before the industrial revolution. But as some avenues were closed, others were opened by the rapid expansion both of higher education and also of scientific training, through universities and colleges of technology—*Technische Hochschulen.* In addition, there were institutions where middle management could find vocational training in either technology or accounting. In Germany more than in most European countries, there were many educational ladders to higher social status, often provided by the State. The respect for learning shown by the broad population, particularly towards "Herr Doktor"—and to "Frau Doktor," his wife, who might never have set foot in a university—was a powerful spur to seek higher education.

Other ladders of social advancement included the army and the civil service, especially when twelve years of military service were followed by an appointment to some petty post in the ever-growing administration—be it in a tax office, or the customs and excise, or within one of the many bureaucracies springing up to regulate industrial life. Konrad Adenauer, the first Chancellor of the Federal Republic of Germany in 1949, was born into the family of a Prussian noncommissioned officer turned customs official. He was sent to the *Gymnasium,* studied law at the university, married into a patrician family and in 1917, when just over forty years old, became mayor of his home town of Cologne. This was, by any standards, an outstanding career. But in the enthusiasm for learning and the iron ambition that it displayed, it was archetypal. Theodor Mommsen, the classicist and recipient of the 1902 Nobel Prize for literature, made an equally exemplary ascent, coming from a north German farmhouse and ending as one of the intellectual luminaries—and most vocal critics—of imperial Germany. Many other such biographies could be added here. Invariably, the background is modest, the bookshelves extensive; the *Gymnasium* is the first step, the university the second, and from there the commanding heights are in sight. Statistics showing that all the senior generals and top administrators were nobles is misleading, since ennoblement, as a rule, came with a certain rank, just as senior British generals and civil servants receive a knighthood today.

Once the Prussian King, by annexing Frankfurt in 1866, had Baron von Rothschild among his subjects, bankers, even Jewish ones, could expect to be promoted to a simple "Von" or a "Freiherr." Abraham Oppenheim, a Jewish banker from Cologne who was of great repute and did many good works, became a Freiherr, and so did Gerson Bleichröder, whose supreme merit was to have vastly augmented Bismarck's fortune. The society of *fin de siècle* Germany was as open to merit, wealth and learning as those of Austria, Belgium and Britain, and certainly more so than that of France.

Women had to wait for the Great War to knock down the fences preventing their full participation in life. It was only after 1900 that women from a middle-class background—the upper crust regarded study as beneath their dignity—set foot in a university as proper students. Some years before the war, not only philosophy and sociology but also the medical sciences were opened to female students. Among the women of the poorer classes, work had been a necessity, not a matter of rights. While the men went out to do the heavy jobs in, for example, the metal industry, the women would stitch and sew in a nearby textile factory, the indispensable grandmother looking after the children. In the artisan world, women had always done the bookkeeping, looking after the wider family and fighting with the authorities. There was no change whatsoever in the pattern of their lives, merely more of the same.

Berlin became the political capital, in defiance of the visceral feeling of many Germans in the west, in the south and in Saxony. "We fear a metropolis," Goethe allows his hero to say in *Wilhelm Meisters Wanderjahre,* referring to Berlin. Indeed, Goethe only visited Berlin himself once or twice in his life and was not amused. After the Congress of Vienna in 1815, the German Confederation made its diplomatic headquarters in the baroque sandstone palace of the Princes of Thurn and Taxis in Frankfurt. In 1848 the revolutionary parliament held its meetings in Frankfurt's Paulskirche, until disbanded, humiliated and relegated to the margins of history. Berlin, meanwhile, epitomized a more successful face of German history, becoming the capital of the German customs union in 1834 simply because Prussia was the proponent of free trade in Germany, while Austria was backward, protectionist and always close to bankruptcy. Prussia was by far the most potent economic player among the German states, enjoying healthy finances, a solid silver and gold currency, and a well-organized tax administration. People in the north German Free Cities, in Cologne or in the south German provinces may not have liked having Berlin as capital, but Bismarck certainly did not care to ask them. He may have treated the princes with exquisite politeness, but there was never any doubt where the real seat of power lay.

Berlin was not merely the new capital, but also the largest industrial center on the Continent. It had the advantage of being at the confluence of the Havel and the Spree rivers, within the vast, flat and sandy landscape that was dominated by the river Elbe. But it was also close to the Oder river farther east. Berlin was also the most important center on the international railway system between Paris and Moscow, Copenhagen and Milan. The Cologne-Minden railway, completed soon after 1848, linked western Germany to Berlin, crossing all the major rivers of northern Germany and continuing, once Berlin was left behind, for another 500 miles to the easternmost ports and garrison towns in East Prussia. Unlike in Munich to the south in Bavaria, where the royal administration had always tried to slow down industrial development in order to preserve peace and quiet, in Berlin industry had always been prominent, strongly supported by the Prussian state administration so as to create employment and generate tax revenue. There was a conscious effort, in a country where only sand was in ample supply, to encourage the industrial arts, to make the *Technische Hochschule* in Charlottenburg a source of advanced technology, to import industrial know-how from Lancashire and Birmingham, and capital from London. The Protestant work ethic, established by French Huguenots fleeing the religious persecution of Louis XIV, together with home-grown pietism and puritanism, nurtured a spirit of enterprise in Berlin.

After 1815 the architect Karl Friedrich Schinkel's Berlin took shape: apart from some Gothic fantasies, it was rigidly neoclassical. Nearly all the Prussian rulers were devoted builders, so Berlin, compared to Vienna, never lost a certain *nouveau* air because it was forever being torn down and redesigned. The city grew from a population of about 200,000 in 1800 to nearly 4 million by 1900, as people left their villages in the east looking for a better and freer life. West Germans did not feel attracted to Berlin, but for the easterners it held great promise, especially for the Jews living in the Russian-controlled parts of Poland. Rosa Luxemburg came from a rabbinical family of the east European Stetl to attend university in Berlin, before transforming herself into a socialist firebrand. Max Liebermann, the most sought-after painter in Berlin at the turn of the century, with a mansion by the Brandenburg Gate and a villa on the Wannsee, also came from the east. The huge industrial companies there offered great opportunities. Borsig made railway engines, Siemens produced telegraph equipment and, later, AEG manufactured electrical appliances. When Bismarck became Prime Minister of Prussia in 1862, he defiantly stated that the great issues of the day would be settled not by speeches and majority voting, but through "blood and iron." The economist John Maynard Keynes corrected him when he observed, seventy-five years later, that German unification had been effected through coal and steel. It was in Berlin that all this energy converged.

At the turn of the century, Berlin was the unchallenged centerpiece of this bustling, optimistic, magnetic—in fact, revolutionary—phenomenon, German industry. Berlin was also the hub of Germany's financial services. After Frankfurt had been occupied by Prussian troops in 1866, demanding a hefty sum in reparations for the city's mistake in supporting Austria, it did not recover for decades. But in fact Frankfurt had already by then failed to grasp the implications of the new industrial world of big business with its joint-stock companies and joint-stock banks. The first of these banks, protecting its masters against the unlimited risks involved in setting up railway companies and the like, was the Darmstädter Bank, founded by an international consortium led by Sal Oppenheim Jr. & Cie of Cologne. It soon gravitated to Berlin, to be close to the seat of power and industry, as did the Disconto Gesellschaft, the Dresdner Bank, the Commerzbank and many others, while the Deutsche Bank began there. The Berlin stock exchange was the German leader and, after 1873, the Reichsbank added further to the city's financial importance. Russian loans were managed from there for the next twenty years, as was the trade of the entire Baltic region, and much investment in both North and South America.

The Berlin of Bismarck was much closer to the London of Palmerston and the Paris of Adolphe Thiers than to the loud, gaudy, neurotic Berlin of the Weimar years after 1919, let alone the brutal *Reichshauptstadt* of the Nazi era. It may have been a powerhouse at the heart of the Continent, but it was also a collection of villages redolent with that atmosphere which Berliners call their *Kiez*—a sense of local community. It combined the arcadian beauty of the Potsdam parks and palaces with the *gravitas* of Germany's foremost university, and levels of enterprise more usually associated with America. There was a willingness to give to patriotic causes, whether the National Gallery sponsored by Crown Prince Frederick William, the Kaiser Wilhelm Gesellschaft for big science that Kaiser William II promoted, or the vast museum complex under the great artistic panjandrum Wilhelm von Bode. After one generation, even the most skeptical had to admit that Berlin, while representing the worst of modern Germany in its urban squalor, exploitation and organized crime, also showed off the best in the arts, industry, banking, architecture and town planning, not to mention health care, transport and infrastructure.

With the exception of the *Frankfurter Zeitung*, Germany's *Financial Times* of the day, all the important newspapers were published in Berlin, often bringing out two or three editions daily, and reporting the Reichstag debates in great detail. This was a lively, nervously aggressive and undeferential media world, concentrated in Kochstrasse just to the south of the political square mile represented by Friedrichstrasse, Wilhelmstrasse and Unter den Linden, between Schlossplatz and Pariser Platz, near the Brandenburg Gate. All the major pressure groups and organized interests set up headquarters in Berlin, channeling information, lobbying, dispensing money, throwing parties and publishing pamphlets that few would ever care to read. They came into their own when free trade gave way to protectionism as a result of the great depression starting in 1873. The argument about state intervention, closely linked to the new Reich's need for revenue, drew new lines not only across the economy, but also across the party system. Bismarck was masterful in his management and manipulation of the many alliances between politics and business, and all of this took place between the Chancellor's office in the Wilhelmstrasse, the Adlon Hotel on Pariser Platz, the Hotel Esplanade and two or three fashionable restaurants like Borchardt's and Lutter & Wegener on Gendarmenmarkt. The Bismarckian system, often described as bordering on autocracy, was as much a matter of lobby politics as any to be found in other industrial nations—France, Belgium, Great Britain or the United States.

Many felt overwhelmed by the speed of change, and not a few feared that the breathless march of life and politics in Berlin was putting at risk everything that had been won. But there were many more who shared the feeling of optimism that prevailed throughout Europe, buoyed up by industrial growth, colonial expansion and a rise in the standard of living. It was when that same mood slipped over into a feeling of unbridled strength that the real danger beckoned.

"The statesman must be a pessimist," Konrad Adenauer once observed, reflecting upon the rise and fall of imperial Germany. "Dangers are looming in every corner." But this was not the mood in Germany at the height of the industrial revolution, when Bismarck seemed to be in control of the European system and when every day widened the horizons of power, the sciences, and industry. History, for once, seemed to be allied with the Germans, and no ghosts were allowed to attend the party.

4

THE WILHELMINE ERA

The Bismarckian endgame was full of drama and futility. It began in 1889, not center-stage in Berlin, but in Upper Silesia and the Ruhr where around 150,000 miners went on strike for higher wages and better accident protection. The army's coal reserves were threatened, so Bismarck wanted to encircle the mines with troops and declare a state of emergency. Kaiser William II, advised by Oberpräsident Baron von Berlepsch who sympathized with the miners' complaints, wanted nothing of the sort. Instead he received a workers' delegation and promised to take up the matter—a wise move, but an insult openly directed against Bismarck and his political system of repression, drama and deterrence.

In addition, the Reichstag elections in the spring of 1890 went badly for the Bismarckians: they lost their parliamentary majority. Serious debate began in the public press, at the court and in the Reichstag, about discontinuing the anti-socialist law, which Bismarck wanted to keep, while the Kaiser, industry and the generals were all for giving up, since it had only served to get the socialists more sympathy and, what was worse, an ever increasing number of votes. The Kaiser adopted a sanctimonious tone, saying, "I do not wish to stain my reign with the blood of my subjects." To force the decision, Bismarck studied ways to engineer a *coup d'état* from above, a pre-emptive strike against the socialists, suspending parliamentary government. The Chancellor's office was instructed to prepare a new military bill and, in addition, an enhanced version of the anti-socialist law. All this might result in turmoil, but it would merely make the old captain that much more indispensable.

This was too much. The Kaiser saw Bismarck no longer as the solution but as the problem, and asked for his resignation. The old man, forever the master of tactics, made it sound as if great issues of foreign policy had been at stake, even war with Russia. But there is no doubt that Bismarck was out of step, that this time the young Kaiser had more wisdom than the old Chancellor, and that most people gave a sigh of relief on the news coming out of Berlin. The Dowager Empress Frederick, Queen Victoria's daughter, welcomed Bismarck's fall as if a new day was dawning:

> How we suffered under that régime! How his influence corrupted a whole school—his staff, Germany's political life! He made life in Berlin almost unbearable if one did not wish to become his depraved slave! His party, his followers and admirers are fifty times worse than he is himself . . . It will take years to undo all the damage done. He who only sees the outside thinks that Germany is strong, great and united, with a huge army . . . If only the price were known that all this has cost.

History, over the years, has been kinder to Bismarck, his fragile system of alliances better understood, his sense of equilibrium vindicated, his achievements shining out in contrast with William II's vainglorious brinkmanship, let alone Hitler's nihilism. His pessimism about Germany and the Germans had always been profound. One evening he told his guests that sleep gave him no respite: "I continue to dream my waking thoughts. Recently I saw the map of Germany in front of my eyes, with one rotten patch after the other peeling off." Or, some years later: "This people does not know how to conduct itself. The propertied do not work. Only the hungry ones are assiduous, and they will devour us." His achievements did not spring from the fact that he was in tune with his age, but rather that he was against it; his dearest wish, after he had saved Prussia's *ancien régime,* was to stop history in its stride. But it was only through a revolution from above of his own making that he could have his wish granted—and then only for a time. Even revolutions from above are, ultimately, revolutions.

When societies change their fundamental *modus operandi,* it is rarely announced in the marketplace. Not so in Germany in 1890. After twenty-eight years at the helm Bismarck was dismissed by his imperial master, William II. This marked not only a dramatic change of generations, but also contained the message that the social fabric of Germany was in the midst of deep and irreversible change. In terms of investment, numbers employed and value of goods produced, industrial output overtook agriculture, with the small but rapidly expanding service sector—banks, insurance, education, civil service, etc.—catching up.

Bismarck's successor, Leo von Caprivi, had been a general in charge of the Admiralty. He was keenly aware, like Bismarck, that an unspoken condition of Germany's continuing security was never to challenge British naval supremacy, but rather to cultivate Britain as a vital makeweight in the European balance of power. Therefore his first step in foreign policy, apart from letting slip the contentious Reinsurance Treaty with Russia, was to follow his own precept of "the less Africa, the better." He exchanged the island of Zanzibar, off the coast of east Africa, much desired by the British, for the island of Heligoland, in the middle of the Elbe estuary—a red rock of considerable strategic importance for Germany. But Germany's fervently rightwing colonial lobby did not appreciate this wisdom. The Pan-German League sprang to life and became the voice of Germany's most vicious nationalism, well endowed with money and media influence.

Caprivi had a keen sense of social equilibrium and also took on the protectionist alliance of *Rittergut und Hochofen,* the blast furnace and the landed estate. He negotiated the commercial treaty with Russia that Bismarck had constantly refused even to consider—at the cost of losing what remained of Russian sympathies; especially among the landowning classes. For Caprivi, a Prussian general turned Reich Chancellor, it was a vital operation, both for security and for trade, to open the German market to imports from Russia and beyond and in turn to access foreign markets hitherto closed. He introduced the draft treaty with Russia in the Reichstag with the argument: "We have to export. Either we export human beings or we export our products. With this constant increase in population, without an equal increase in industry we cannot live." Caprivi was keenly aware that the German balance of trade with the world had been constantly in the red for more than a decade. He also understood that, given Germany's geostrategic situation, domestic rifts could not be allowed to widen. After the anti-socialist law had been abandoned, the Reich administration tried to integrate the trade unions into the body politic of Germany, inviting representatives of organized labor to sit on industrial courts and promoting the self-governing system of mandatory social insurance that helped to bind German society together. In this, for once, Caprivi followed in the footsteps of Bismarck, who had realized that Germany's precarious position in Europe made it imperative to preserve social peace at home and pay the price of the rapidly expanding welfare state.

But all of this did not endear the general-turned-Chancellor to the protectionist lobby, the nationalist organizations and court society. The landed interest created the Reichslandbund within less than a year, an organization of more than 300,000 card-carrying members, openly declaring that they would learn from the socialists how to agitate, that they would carry their complaints "to the steps of the throne" and that they wanted Caprivi out. William II gave way, Caprivi had to go, and immediately work began to revise the tariffs, which were to reach a new high in 1902 amidst continuing protest from industry. The Caprivi interlude (1890–94)—with its steps towards integrating the working classes and their organizations into political life, accommodating the expanding role of German export industries, changing the climate from Bismarckian confrontation to compromise and practicing *détente* policies abroad—begs the question of whether industrial Germany could not have become, instead of an uncertain giant, the centerpiece of European stability well into the new century.

In economic and industrial terms, the twentieth century had started long before 1899. With electricity providing a clean and cheap source of energy, a new wave of industrialization swept through the 1890s. It transformed not only the factory floor but also, thanks to electric trams or trains, above and under ground, the faces of cities and the way people organized their lives by day or lit them by night. The house of Siemens, founded by a former first lieutenant in the Prussian Signals Corps, started as a family company in the early days of the telegraph but later, through its intimate alliance with Deutsche Bank, turned into a worldwide operation. Telegraph technology was the foundation of the business, and Siemens was a leader in creating land-based and sea-based cable connections, introducing instant communications to facilitate commerce, strategy and politics. Later, Siemens concentrated on the supply side of the electrical industry. Emil Rathenau's AEG, having started as a licensee of the Edison patents, focused on the demand side—the transformation of daily life through washing machines, electrical stoves and kettles, refrigerators, irons, etc. Rathenau engaged Peter Behrens, the architect, in 1907. As well as building factories without any reference to former styles, Behrens applied a sober and functional style, owing nothing to the pre-industrial past, to the new equipment that replaced millions of household servants and profoundly changed everyday life.

At the turn of the century, the Germans were no longer taking the boat to the New World, but were trying to make a better living in the cities than their forefathers had on the land. Germany was not a land of unlimited opportunity, like the United States of legend, but by European standards it came very close: the collective biography would show not only an abstract rise in income, but also that people consumed more soap, more beef, more wine, more white bread, more shirts and more shoes than ever before. More books were read by a population in which illiteracy was waning, and more newspapers were consumed. The anger of the old, Bismarckian days was largely overcome; even the anger of socialists and Catholics, the one-time *Reichsfeinde*. When the twentieth century dawned, it was, by any standards, Germany's *belle époque*—an Edwardian age full of energy and optimism, with Cassandra muted and outside the city gates. This century could have been, French philosopher Raymond Aron once observed, the

German century. Many Germans at its beginning were entitled to hope so.

What mattered to the great majority of people throughout the German lands was not high politics but daily life, the inexorable changes accompanying it and the ever more painful question of whether yesterday's experience could be a guide to tomorrow's challenges. In most cases the answer was a clear no, which in turn called into question the relationship of father and son, of mother and daughter, of husband and wife. Compared to this, what did it matter who was in charge in Berlin, what the Reichstag did or failed to do, or what the Kaiser had to say about the German battle fleet, perfidious Albion or colonial adventures in faraway places like Kiao-Chau in China, Swakopmund in southwest Africa, or Samoa in the Pacific? Herr und Frau Müller or Schmidt had to get on with their daily lives, make a living and get acquainted with the new technologies that were changing almost every trade, every shop, every business—in fact, all the accepted coordinates of people's lives. Tradition, in spite of all the crowns, the eagles and the lions still proudly displayed on the coinage, on public buildings and on official documents, was eroding day by day. Of course, in rural Pomerania; East Prussia or West Prussia and in the mountains of Franconia or in Upper Bavaria, many hours by train away from old and new industrial centers, daily life looked much as it had for many generations past. But that was not where money, progress, a career and freedom of choice beckoned. Small towns like Rothenburg ob der Tauber, because the railway from Würzburg to Augsburg bypassed them, began to live in a time warp of medieval houses and marketplaces, while the children insisted that there was no breathing space in the quaint old place. Never were the Germans more enthusiastic about the promise of technology, progress and the future than at the turn of the century.

A traveller having traversed the thousand miles of Reichsstrasse I from Aachen via Potsdam and Berlin, all the way to Königsberg in East Prussia in 1870, and repeating that experience thirty-five or even forty years later, would have seen a country fundamentally changed: railways and telegraph lines almost everywhere, the trains carrying not only people, but huge quantities of industrial goods. From time to time, when an aircraft might be seen overhead, children would point it out to each other and vow one day to try and fly themselves. Perhaps there might be a motorcar on the road, driven by an enterprising young man with a lot of money. Most roads, sand or dirt in the old days, would now be paved. In the cities, electric tramcars would now link the center with faraway villages, which were rapidly turning into suburbs for an ever-increasing army of office clerks. The better suburbs would have villas in an extensive, parklike landscape, lit by electric light, where fifty years ago there had been, at best, some modest huts and a small church. Rivers would be crossed by elegant steel bridges, while canals linked the Rhine to the Weser, the Weser to the Elbe, and the Elbe to the Oder— the whole north German plain became on interconnected system of waterways, with its center in Berlin. Rivers had been made navigable during the last few decades; the Lorelei Rock celebrated by Heinrich Heine, and a danger to shipping on the Rhine, had finally been blown up. But the long-projected canal from the Main river across the hills of Franconia to the Danube had yet to be completed. The most conspicuous difference would have been people. The children of the poor were no longer barefoot, begging for something to eat; instead they went to primary and secondary school, later into industrial or artisan apprenticeships, later still into the army and then on into a middle-class way of life, possibly helped by some technical education.

However, when those customs and traditions that have governed people's lives for centuries die, there is bound to be anxiety and fear of the future. The world was not becoming any more reassuring as myths fell apart, taboos were dismissed and the boundaries of human thought and action were daily breached. This outbreak of energy, technological and human, was coupled with a feeling of *fin de siècle* decadence, that there was a price to be paid and nowhere more so than in the writings of Friedrich Nietzsche, who was dying a slow death. The head of Janus in Greek mythology, representing old and young, the past and the future, but also the pain of the fleeting moment, could have been the symbol of Germany's—and for that matter Europe's—destiny at the turn of the century. It was in the visionary world of literature and the arts that this ambiguity found its foremost expression; among poets, artists, architects, engineers and scientists. At no other time could Thomas Mann's epic novel *Die Buddenbrooks* have been written, the saga of the decline and fall of a patrician family from Lübeck. At about the same time, Walther Rathenau, an outsider among Jews as well as Germans, set out to write his visionary *Von kommenden Dingen*— the shape of things to come.

In 1889 Otto Brahm, Maximilian Harden, Theodor Wolff (publisher of the liberal *Berliner Tageblatt* newspaper) and the Hart brothers set up the Freie Volksbühne—literally, the "free popular stage"—to avoid censorship. Their model was the Théâtre libre in Paris, set up by André Antoine. The same year, Gerhard Haupt-mann's *Vor Sonnenaufgang* was staged for the first time, with its strong message of social discontent. The result was a public scandal, but this only served to add publicity to the undertaking and to give a second wind to Ibsen's and Zola's naturalistic drama and fiction, which aimed for social, even scientific, truth through representing the daily life of ordi-nary people. In their wake at the turn of the century came Arno Holz's *Die Sozialaristokraten*—about the noble poor, reflecting some earlier ideas of Benjamin Disraeli in *Sybil: Or the Two Nations* (1845). *Meister Oelze* by Johannes Schlaf broadcast a similar message; so did *Die Ehre* by Sudermann, *Jugend*—"Youth"—by Max Halbe and dramas by Otto Erich Hartleben and Karl Schönherr. The greatest scandal came with Gerhard Hauptmann's *Die Weber* about the mis-ery of mid-nineteenth-century weavers in Silesia and the greed of the capitalist entrepreneur. The police saw this as a provocation, upsetting public order, and their Berlin chief, Baron Bernhard von Richthofen, banned it. So it was performed privately by the Freie Volksbühne and attracted considerable attention. One year later, a court allowed it to be played in public and it was met with much applause, turning the performance and the reaction of the public into an unmistakable demonstration against the Kaiser's art criticism. His Majesty, also supreme commander of the army and navy, retaliated by letting it be known that offi-cers should not attend, certainly not wearing uniform, and he canceled his box. What happened in Berlin was repeated in other places, like Schwabing in Munich where the cabaret adopted a sharp and bitter tone. The weekly magazines *Jugend,* for lifestyle, and *Simplicissimus,* for polit-ical satire, both became great popular successes. The first catered to the dreamland of youthful misfits, creating the floral and romantic German version of Art Nouveau called Jugendstil. The other mocked the establishment, with uniform or without, to the amusement of many of its members. Both journals confirmed the Munich public's conviction that the middle classes, especially the south German variety, were better human beings than the monocled officers and the stuffy Prussian bureaucrats from Berlin. The cartoons and accompanying articles in the *Simpl,* as it was called, were biting and showed rifts that officially were not allowed to exist.

A new, lighter lifestyle was emerging in suburbia, normally labelled *belle époque,* but in Munich known as *Prinzregentenzeit,* after the Bavarian prince regent who, having succeeded the exotic but mad King Ludwig II, lived an openly relaxed life between Munich and Berchtesgaden and was very popular. A wave of alienation swept middle-class youths, who found official Germany, especially in its Prussian variety, both ridiculous and deplorable. A radical chic also emerged, idealistic more than hedonistic, among young men and women who loved themselves and the art world and who felt pity for the strict conventions of their parents. For them decadence was not a menace but a new, soft and sensitive form of life.

To be young was not only, as in the past, a passing phase en route to a career, but a way of life and a *Weltanschauung* embracing a willingness to challenge all accepted wisdom and most certainly to defy any lessons that uneasy parents might have to offer. The youth movement would not stay at home, but rather went out to seek nature, singing a farewell to the stuffy world left behind in the narrow cities while enjoying a free life on the mountains. They were serious young men and women together, singing, reading, reciting the poet Rilke's *Kornett* and, for the rest of the night, doing what young men and women have always done. They made pilgrimages to the Hoher Meissner, a mountain out of the tales of the brothers Grimm near Cassel in Hesse. In 1913 thousands of students came together there, professing their idealism and promising each other *innere Wahrhaftigkeit*—truthfulness—and never to become like their parents. They saw themselves as an elite, called upon to create a new land for a new era. Instead it was this same generation of *Wandervogel* and *Jugendbewegung* that only one year later, singing "Deutschland Deutschland über alles," went to die in Flanders' fields.

Of the many new avenues to a better future, none was more exciting and revolutionary than the discovery of sexuality and its unexplored wonderland. For centuries, the attraction of men and women to the opposite sex had been something never to be mentioned, and was depicted only in terms of gods courting goddesses or shepherds flirting with innocent shepherdesses—something that was part of God's great creation, but outside the conventions of polite society. The Viennese psychiatrist Dr. Sigmund Freud took the ground from under the establishment itself, eroding its rigid standards of marriage, parenthood, property and conjugal fidelity. Suddenly, men and women were facing each other in an unforgiving but also seductive light. They did not have to read psychiatric journals to understand that vast changes were in the air. The fundamental message was one of liberation, but the defenders of tradition sounded a note of caution, pointing at the price to be paid in terms of human unhappiness and frustration. What seduced people also undermined civil society, and linked to the exciting news about sexuality there was also an ominous hint about the role of violence. Moreover, if people were driven by forces inside themselves and beyond their control, what would happen to the age-old notions of responsibility, accountability and morality? The pillars of society were beginning to shake. What would happen to marriage, to time-honored institutions built upon the suppression of sexuality?

In *Tannhäuser* and elsewhere, Richard Wagner's music theater had already, two or three decades before, given serious and disconcerting hints, as the emotions on stage corresponded to the sound and fury from the orchestra. This music signaled the end of all conventions, but still coded it in a language of an ancient, mythological past. But the scandalous, subversive message was there to be seen and heard by those who, every year, made the pilgrimage to the festival of Bayreuth. Bismarck, by denying to Bayreuth a subvention from the Reich budget, had shown a fine instinct that Wagner's music encouraged more dangerous upheaval than many of the socialist speeches delivered in the Reichstag.

Theodor Fontane, through many graphic descriptions in his "Wanderungen durch die Mark Brandenburg," sang the praises of the Prussian nobility and idealized their country seats. But he was also, in his novels, a sensitive observer of how moral standards were being eroded by the constant struggle of emotions, recently liberated, against the established class structure. In *Effi Briest* the heroine is cruelly punished when her illicit admirer is killed in a duel. *Stine* tells the sad story of a love affair that cuts across social barriers, and so does *Irrungen Wirrungen.* Fontane allowed his characters to suffer and to fail in their futile, premature pursuit of happiness. But Ibsen and Strindberg, among the following generation, were more aggressive and found fault not so much with the frailty of the human soul as with the rigidity of worn-out conventions. What Flaubert did to Madame Bovary and Tolstoy to Anna Karenina—that is, turning those heroic fools for love into casualties in a deadly struggle—found daily expression in lives up and down Europe, and most certainly in Germany. People had tasted the bittersweet fruit of knowledge and were now facing a world that was neither hell nor heaven, but defied every conventional wisdom.

Moral ambiguity became the keynote of modern times. Equipped with the knowledge afforded by modern science and troubled by doubt in God's existence, and so in his own destiny, man was failing to find easy answers to the great questions. Ibsen, Strindberg, Hauptmann and Chekhov were all asking for the ultimate meaning of the human condition, but were finding nothing but shaking walls and cracked façades. In Tchaikovsky's *Nutcracker* the rats conquer the white knights, while St. Petersburg's court society gave its applause. Wedekind's *Frühling's Erwachen* and Arthur Schnitzler's *Der Reigen* became more specific and were regularly banned, which only made them more fascinating. They presented a sophisticated web of cynicism, hypocrisy, frigidity and empty desire—with love and warmth as the victims. Richard Strauss in *Salome* took away the last veils of the past. What was to be discovered, off stage, were the unknown lands of the human soul. As they were explored, they revealed an infinite recession of labyrinthine strongholds. Poets and psychologists, however, were not to blame for what followed. They did no more than give expression to the upheavals in the collective soul of Europe.

5

EUROPE–A CONCERT NO MORE

The repose of Europe, as British statesmen of the early decades of the nineteenth century used to describe the balance of power, had been rudely disturbed by the national and social revolutions of 1830 and 1848 all over Europe. Ever since, the foundations of power and legitimacy had been shaky.

Governments and regimes now had to prove, not their ancient lineage but their effectiveness in dynamic nation-states, providing jobs, raising incomes and harnessing modern industry to the needs of society. Rising populations and the quickening pace of industrialization made it imperative to secure raw materials and to open markets. The new mood from the Bristol Channel to the wetlands of the Vistula was a constant forward flight to produce consensus within societies driven by class conflict at home and competition abroad. Germany was no exception.

In 1871 the British government watched, with some unease, how the balance on the Continent was forcefully rearranged through the German triumph over France. While the war was being wound up, Benjamin Disraeli gave expression to deep-seated anxieties about the implications of what had happened on the European continent in the course of the last decade. He termed it "the German revolution," betraying through this term that the events defied traditional British statesmanship and balance of power politics.

Disraeli had looked far into the future but subsequent British governments, including his own, took a much more relaxed view of the new Germany. When, as Lord Beaconsfield and Prime Minister, he attended the Berlin Congress in 1878, he appreciated Bismarck's performance, and Bismarck returned the compliment saying, "Der alte Jude, das ist der Mann." Her Majesty's Government, concerned about the Great Game in central Asia against the Russians who were advancing towards India, as well as with French meddling in Africa, much appreciated Germany's mediating role at the Congo Conference convoked in Berlin in 1884 to delineate borders. Bismarck and his British counterparts, however, never found enough common ground to come to a formal understanding. Bismarck feared what he called "a German Gladstone cabinet" and did everything to prevent it. To him, and to the social milieu he came from, parliamentary government was a contradiction in terms, parliaments invariably being seen as divided, weak and incapable of organizing national strength. Germany's exposed position in the center of Europe gave an added argument for keeping ultimate control in the hands of a military monarchy. But regardless of differences in philosophy and power structure, the silent alliance between Britain and Germany worked well under Bismarck and for a few years after. The dynastic ties between the House of Hohenzollern and the House of Hanover looked like a promise of partnership throughout Europe and the world. Queen Victoria, "Grandmother of Europe," was also the grandmother of Crown Prince William, who came to the throne in 1888.

By the time Bismarck had to leave the Chancellor's office in 1890, France and Russia were working to forge an alliance in both commercial and military terms. French capital markets were supplying Russian industrialization with the investment that was drying up, not least thanks to Bismarck's intervention, from the German side. The

French arms industry looked to provide the Russian armies with modern equipment. Russian officers were lavishly entertained in Paris, and naval squadrons paid much-heralded visits to Le Havre and St. Petersburg. This was the "nightmare" that Bismarck had always feared, posing a threat to Germany's strategic borders in the west and to Austria's existence in the east. Now more than ever was the time to cultivate Germany's informal alliance with the British Empire. But such a strategic collaboration rested on one overriding condition: that Germany continued to honor traditional Prussian restraint in naval matters. The German navy had been the most tangible expression of German national aspirations during the revolutionary months of 1848, and the few ships acquired were auctioned off when that episode ended. The army remained firmly under the control of the monarchy, while the navy was an expression of middle-class and commercial ambition, destined for wider horizons than the old battlefields in Poland and Champagne where the scions of the Prussian aristocracy had spilled their blood. The footguard and horseguard officers of Potsdam looked upon it as a costly and money-consuming vehicle for ambitious technocrats and *Etagen-Adel*, landless nobles. For Bismarck the few cruisers under the black, white and red colors of the Reich had no purpose except to fly such flags and transport troops. To underline traditional priorities, an infantry general was put in charge of the navy. But with the arrival of William II, given to romantic dreams of naval grandeur, wishing to impress his British cousins and, if possible, put them into second place, all this was to change.

William II had a kind of love-hate relationship with Britain, its empire and in particular with the Royal Navy, which he saw in all its splendor on his annual visits to

Cowes, next door to Portsmouth. He believed like many of his middle-class subjects that Germany's expanding global trade required for its protection a blue-water deep-sea navy. Sir Ernest Cassel—a close friend of the Prince of Wales, the future Edward VII—and Albert Ballin, chief of the Hamburg Amerika Line and often the Kaiser's dinner guest, both knew more about shipping than anybody else and tried to persuade hotheads on both sides to moderate their views, but in vain. There was loose talk about British commercial envy, although Britain kept faith with free trade long after Germany had converted to protectionism. The fact that there were many advances in naval architecture and technology about this time whetted appetites: the torpedo, the steam turbine engine, better armor, better guns, better optics, the imminent prospect of submarines, of oil replacing coal as fuel. Did this not give the energetic newcomer all the chances in the world to outflank the established supremacy of the Royal Navy?

A youthful and energetic naval captain called Alfred Tirpitz, from a modest but ambitious middle-class family in the north, found his vocation in devising a battle fleet for the Kaiser capable of forcing the British into a strategic duel where their empire was most vulnerable, in the waters around the British Isles. Such a strategy was in blatant defiance of the time-honored instincts of the Junkers, with their great respect for the combined might of Russia and France. What fascinated the Kaiser, however, was the chance to impress not only British admirals but also German voters, and to capture their imagination and loyalty by opening up new prospects for Germany's *Grosse Politik*. He saw himself as a true successor of the "soldier king" Frederick William I and his son Frederick the Great, and wanted to go down as another hero in the annals of Prussian greatness. The army may have felt that this was no time to divert funds to a navy that no sensible person could really desire, but it did not understand the fascination of distant colonies and naval displays for the middle classes of Germany.

Naval fever among the Germans owed much to the wave of imperialism gripping the world in the 1880s. In 1882 the scramble for Africa began when the British Empire, on top of controlling the Suez Canal through a majority shareholding, formally occupied Egypt. Other European powers looked for acquisitions elsewhere. Bismarck, meanwhile, kept a cool head. One day a colonial adventurer came to impress upon him the need to catch up with France and Britain and to stake out German claims in Africa. "Your map of Africa is very nice," Bismarck said. "But there is France, and here is Russia, and we are in the middle, and that is my map of Africa." However, pressure from the press and the public mounted, driven by the idea that vast riches waited to be grabbed by German explorers and traders, and that, if emigration from German lands could not be stopped, at least it should be channeled into German colonies.

Reluctantly, Bismarck accepted that a little money from the Reich budget should be allocated for subsidies to shipping lines, and that the German flag should be raised in Tanganyika in east Africa, where tea and coffee could be grown, and in southwest Africa where diamonds and other desirables were eventually discovered. However, he never lost sight of the precarious position of the Reich in the middle of the European system. He therefore did everything possible to help the French to get enmeshed in Africa and Asia so as to make French public opinion forget *la ligne bleue des Vosges,* and succumb instead to the lure of the Atlas mountains and the rice paddies of Cochinchine. With the British he was willing to swap Zanzibar for Heligoland in the North Sea, and his successor Caprivi delivered. In his last years in office Bismarck, weary of colonial imbroglios with the British Empire, even tried to rid the Reich of the whole colonial burden, negotiating with a consortium of Hanseatic merchants who would, for a symbolic rent of one mark, run the show on their own account. Alas, this was not to be. The colonial lobby had grown too strong, the popular fascination with far-flung dependencies too great.

So Germany, after the Caprivi interlude of strategic restraint, continued to plant the black, white and red flag in the South Pacific and on the shores of China. However, even the most fervent of colonial enthusiasts also began to learn that the future lay as much with informal imperialism—trade routes, control of strategic minerals and other precious goods, such as oil, sisal and rubber, and captive markets overseas. British jingoism, French chauvinism and German imperialism matched each other, with the Russians, Italians, Belgians, Japanese and Americans also in the running. The Netherlands, Portugal and Spain had had colonies since the sixteenth century. In a thundering Reichstag speech in 1897, the chief of the Wilhelmstrasse, as the German Foreign Office came to be called, State Secretary Bernhard von Bülow, demanded "a place in the sun." He did not have in mind a picnic spot in the nearby Tiergarten, Berlin's Hyde Park, but foreign possessions to dream about, and from which to make money, to gain prestige and to enhance national cohesion. A German government saying no to the colonial lure would have had to be strong, and not even Bismarck at the zenith of his power had been able to reject completely what he saw as dangerous and entangling adventures. But the successive incum-

bents of the Wilhelmstrasse—from 1894 to 1900 the sep-
tuagenarian Prince Hohenlohe, no longer capable of serious work, and from 1900 to 1909 Baron, then Count and
Prince von Bülow, called by his many detractors "the eel"
because of his extremely flexible spine—were weak leaders. They were appointed by the Kaiser so he could have
all the prestige and glory of *Weltpolitik,* imagining he could
run the country with a combination of neo-absolutism and
charismatic leadership, undisturbed by the complications
of modern industrial society. For William II, the whole of
Germany was nothing but a giant toy created by the
Almighty to please His Imperial Majesty. Of course, this
could never work in a political system with militant organized interests and ambitious and jealous political parties,
and it ended, after a series of gaffes on his part, in sad car-
icature.

The battle fleet and all the vainglorious dreams coming
with it in fact provided a powerful and suggestive means,
not so much for foreign adventure as for domestic consensus. Up and down the country Admiral von Tirpitz, now in
high administrative office as Secretary for the Navy, paid
journalists to sing the praises of imperialism and professors to give *Weltpolitik* their academic blessing. In 1896 Max
Weber, one of the great sociologists of the early twentieth
century and later a democrat by conviction, thundered in
his inaugural lecture at the University of Freiburg that the
founding of the German Empire in 1871 would have been
nothing but a youthful whim if it were not followed, here
and now, by a massive commitment to "a new *Grosse Politik.*" The Flottenverein—the Naval League—was one big
propaganda machine, well oiled by the Reichsmarineamt
and its secret funds. Even opposition members of the
Reichstag were treated with great finesse when it came to

voting ever more funds for a navy whose strategic failure was clear to see by the time the British began building a new fleet of all-big-gun Dreadnought battleships in 1900.

Never was there a political strategy more broadly based and more popularly accepted than the conversion of Germany to the battle fleet. It was founded in the borderlands of democracy and demagoguery, but it also recruited support across a wide array of organized interests. Even the landowning classes were somehow reconciled to the naval enterprise through the return to agricultural protectionism, embodied in the tariffs introduced by Johannes von Miquel, Prussian Minister of Finance. They had acquired a taste for the better things in life, but their estates were mortgaged to the hilt, while they observed with disdain how the rich *Commercienrath* in the city—a title conferred by the administration on the rich, public-minded industrialist or banker, conveying official recognition of merit, sound finances and respectability—could pick a son-in-law from the flower of the aristocracy. In this situation they enjoyed the return to protectionism, recognized the bargain and welcomed a respite in a long story of decline.

The blue 100-mark bill portrayed a well-armed Germania, holding the emblems of commerce and industry, sitting under a giant oak tree, her gaze fixed on a long line of battleships steaming at high speed. At the turn of the century, little boys and girls from the well-to-do families used to wear sailor suits as their Sunday best and there is not a family photo from those days where naval uniform is not to be seen. The naval building program gave employment to the large arms firms such as Krupp of Essen and displayed German workmanship at its most modern, especially in optics and electrical appliances. A special tax was introduced on champagne to help pay for the navy—a tax that, by the way, has survived to this day.

Germany was an industrial latecomer compared to Britain. But in the last decades of the nineteenth century, German industry was catching up rapidly, and after 1900 it was beginning to overtake all of its earlier competitors except the United States of America. German big business, as a rule, harnessed the sciences to its wagon, with the state-financed colleges of technology and *Technische Hochschulen* supplying a steady stream of ambitious, hard-working experts. German companies large and small, not spoiled by captive markets in colonies and dominions, paid more attention to marketing, invested in permanent education for the workforce and understood the economies of scale better than their British competitors. The fusion of basic research and practical application became a specific German strength, while the early shortage of capital had been overcome long ago, not least through the formation of giant, multifunctional banks operating worldwide.

Iron and steel output were an indicator for both economic strength and military potential. Germany forged ahead from 4.1 million tons in 1880 to 6.3 million in 1900 and 17.6 million in 1913, while Britain fell behind significantly: 8.0 million in 1880, 5.0 million in 1900, 7.7 million in 1913. The figures of iron and steel output for the United States are no less instructive: 9.3 million in 1880, 10.3 million in 1900, 31.8 million in 1913. France, Russia, Austria-Hungary and Japan were, by comparison, insignificant, and so was Italy. In energy consumption, another indicator of industrial prowess, Germany started in 1880 at about half the British level, but by 1913 the two countries were almost on a par. In terms of aggregate industrial potential, measured in numbers employed, investment and value of production, Germany had overtaken Britain by 1913, while the United States was a global power in the making. In comparative terms the index was: USA 298.1, Germany 137.7, Britain 127.2.

Military strength and manpower did not keep pace with these industrial figures. In 1880 Germany had 425,000 soldiers and sailors, compared to Russia's 791,000, France's 543,000 and Britain's 367,000. In 1910 the numbers were Germany 694,000, France, with a considerably smaller population, 769,000, Britain 571,000 and the United States 127,000. In warship tonnage, Britain remained the leader throughout, but the margin closed significantly: in 1880 Germany had 88,000 tonnes, Britain 650,000, France 27,000, Russia 200,000 and the United States 169,000. In 1910 the figure was 964,000 tonnes for Germany, while Britain registered 2,174,000, France 725,000, the United States 824,000 and Imperial Japan 496,000. In short, while Germany's steel production led Europe, the country remained far behind in terms of military personnel. Even the substantial increase in naval vessels, in spite of Admiral von Tirpitz's ambitious and long-term building program of 1897, left it with only about 40 per cent of the British overall tonnage.

At the time of the Boer War in southern Africa (1899–1902), the British Foreign Office was ready to contemplate an alliance with "our German cousins," but the Wilhelmstrasse, under pressure from an enraged public, could not oblige. Instead the Franco-British *Entente Cordiale* of 1904 ended Britain's diplomatic and strategic isolation. Originally meant simply to forestall colonial imbroglios between Britain and France, such as the recent one in Upper Egypt near Fashoda, the *Entente Cordiale* was soon seen as a means to contain Germany's expanding power. British leaders had shown for many years that they were no longer able and willing to manage the balance of Europe, yet now they got involved in the system of continental alliances and, unwittingly, put at risk the very empire whose existence they wanted to preserve. This was tragedy for both Britain and Germany.

The German leaders were far from having a strategy to acquire global power, but in London and Paris they were perceived as pursuing a master plan. During the first Morocco crisis in 1905, when the French tightened control over this north African territory, the Kaiser sent a naval detachment to Tangier. He wanted to remind the French that Germany was strong and that Russia, after the Japanese victory in 1904, was weak, and that they had better think of compensations for Germany. At the subsequent Algeciras Conference, Germany did indeed receive another piece of Africa. But the price was that the *Entente Cordiale* was consolidated. In 1907, when Britain and Russia reached agreement over the Far East as well as over Persia and Afghanistan, putting to rest the "Great Game" at least for the time being, Russia became a partner to the *Entente Cordiale*. The resulting Triple Entente reinforced the geostrategic pincer movement on Germany, whose government and people were enraged by this "encirclement." And encirclement it was, unwise by every standard of modern arms control, let alone by traditional old-world diplomacy. But German diplomacy had contributed decisively: "Intoxicated by German power, the Germans felt the need of no allies and made concessions to no one." Whether this is, as A. J. P. Taylor claimed, the one and only meaning of "encirclement" for Germany can be doubted. The European diplomat and historian George F. Kennan in his *Decline of the Bismarckian Order* had a different story: he saw French and Russian policies converging, ever since the 1880s, to undo the status quo, revise the settlement of 1871 and destroy the Habsburg monarchy. The *Entente Cordiale* finally tipped the balance of Europe against the central powers, and thereby the European system became menacingly unstable. In addition, among the central powers Austria-Hungary was seen as a sick man, while the *Entente* could not count on revolution-torn Russia. Both sides therefore had a strange incentive to go to war sooner rather than later, for fear that a member might easily collapse before it could enter the fray.

If the European concert was used to being conducted by the Great Powers, and the Franco-Russian alliance was incompatible with this, so too was German naval ambition. Given Britain's development of the Dreadnought type of battleship, the game on the naval chessboard would have been all but lost for Germany, had it not been for the torpedo boat and the U-boat. The German Admiralty henceforth concentrated on such new types of warship, which offered the chance of victory for the weak over the strong. In 1912 Lord Haldane, then the British Secretary for War, hoped that, given the new correlation of forces, Germany might be willing to sign a naval agreement to limit numbers. In Berlin, however, Haldane met with stiff resistance from Tirpitz and the Kaiser: too much prestige and funds had been invested to retreat and acknowledge defeat. There was to be no arms control. A chance to avoid disaster, perhaps the best chance in decades, was wasted.

German strategy, running into a dead end in naval affairs, could have opted for confidence and security building, returning to Bismarckian wisdom. That would have included limiting arms expenditure either on a contractual basis with Britain or unilaterally, in order to outmaneuver the *Entente Cordiale*. Even the Kaiser, at times, had the good sense to cultivate his Russian cousin, and they met to exchange uniforms and toast each other, as the "Admiral of the Atlantic" and the "Admiral of the Pacific." Pre-1914 Europe was not on a one-way road to disaster; all was not doom and gloom. The Germans and the British not only managed jointly to contain the vicious Balkan Wars of 1912–13, through a London-based diplomatic conference, but also came to an agreement about how to carve up the Portuguese colonies between them in case Portugal could not service its foreign debt. Even the quarrels over Turkey were brought under control, and a formula was adopted to keep the Russians out while giving naval matters to the British and land matters to the Germans. The latter included the strategic Baghdad railway, which was financed by Deutsche Bank and built by a German consortium led by Mannesmann. It aimed to link the Bosphorus with the Persian Gulf and the Red Sea. The remnants, in many places blown up during World War I or left to silent decay, can still be seen today.

It was an age of strategic ambiguity, not an inevitable collective walk down the infernal grove. But faced with encirclement, the Grosser Generalstab in Berlin was unnerved and reacted in a professional but utterly undiplomatic and ultimately fatal way. After the wars of German unification under the leadership of Field Marshal Count Moltke, a legend in his own time, German strategy recognized France as the foremost potential enemy. Officially, Russia was an ally even if the Prussians never really dropped their eastern guard. But the concepts of war in the west and war in the east were kept neatly apart so as to allow the political leaders strategic options at a time of crisis.

After 1900, however, after the invention of the battle fleet, German strategic thinking took another fatal turn. The Franco-Russian military alliance of the last decade had by now become an established fact, celebrated through military exchanges and reinforced by steady Russian arms procurement from French companies. French capital markets continued to provide loans for the cash-strapped state and investment in Russian industry (earning 1 per cent above normal market rates). The combined strength of the Tsar's and the Third Republic's armies by far outnumbered the central powers' forces. In this situation, the Prussian Generalstab under Count Schlieffen decided that any future war would have to be fought on two fronts, against France and Russia, and at almost the same time.

What came to be called the "Schlieffen Plan," was a strategy without any alternative, pure technocratic hubris, and a recipe for defeat. Had not the older Moltke always taught his disciples that no plan could outlast the first encounter with the enemy? In 1905 German strategy was finally built on the assumption that the French were fast in their mobilization and the Russians slow. Therefore, irrespective of the causes of war, hostilities would have to start with a big lightning offensive in the west, defeating the French armies, taking Paris and dictating peace before the Russian bear had really stirred. Meanwhile, in the east only depleted reserves would be put up against the slow-moving Russians, making use of the fortress of Posen, of the rivers and the marshes of these lowlands, and doing their best to hold the Oder line. Subsequently, victory in the west having been achieved, the German armies, swiftly moving by railway, would throw their might against the Russian masses, inflict decisive defeat on them and save the Austro-Hungarian armies from being crushed. Presented as a master plan, in reality this was a strategy born out of despair and bound to lead to disaster.

Germany's neighbors may have found the country's recent appearance at the strategic center of the Continent deeply unsettling. After Bismarck, the implications were also too much for the Germans themselves.

6

BRINKSMANSHIP

Not everyone in Europe was sleepwalking to Armageddon in the years prior to 1914. In his book of 1899, *Is War Now Impossible?*, a Warsaw financier called Ivan Stanizlosovich Block predicted stalemate and trench warfare because of developments in military technology. In Britain, Norman Angell, one of Lord Northcliffe's newspaper editors, suggested in *The Great Illusion* (1910) that the model of the British Empire, made up in large part of practically independent states and guaranteeing "trade by free consent," should be adopted by Europe as the solution to "the international problem." In Germany it was Walther Rathenau, more than anyone else, who comprehended the danger of his time and suggested far-sighted methods of avoidance.

Rathenau was a man of many sides—in fact, of vast contradictions, a technocrat, a visionary, a philosopher advocating a cool neoclassical rationalism, a Jewish citizen of the world who would have preferred not to have been a Jew; he was also a Prussian patriot and a designer of electrical networks for the whole of Europe that he thought would render war impossible and waste obsolete. His collected works and letters run to many volumes, written as he was guiding AEG (Allgemeine Elektrizitäts-Gesellschaft), his father's industrial empire, through a period of relentless experimentation and constant expansion.

He regarded Germany's *ancien régime* with both contempt and admiration. He wanted to be separated from it, but at the same time to be part of it. Rathenau's vision of the future was rather a network of industrial democracies forming a united Europe, analogous to the electricity grids constructed by AEG at the turn of the century. This ran counter to the nationalism and imperialism prevailing in Europe and, sensing what was to come in 1914, Rathenau worked on it desperately.

> I see shadows fall wherever I look. I see them when I walk the streets of Berlin in the evening, when I observe the insolence of our maddening wealth; when I listen to the emptiness of vainglorious phrases or hear talk about pseudogermanic exclusivity. An epoch is not in good health just because the lieutenant shines and the attaché is full of hope. Matters are more serious for Germany now than they have been for decades.

Though born with a silver spoon in his mouth, Rathenau studied electrochemistry, so he understood that the steam-driven machinery of the first industrial revolution was being overtaken by the electricity of the second. "Mechanization" was a stage to be overcome, not only to liberate human beings from boring work, but also to allow the processes of modern management and banking to optimize production and distribution. In 1899 he joined the board of AEG, where his responsibility was to finance and construct electrical power plants and to create a Europe-wide network, with AEG in the center. The overcapacity hitting the electrical markets in 1900 was for him nothing but an incentive to reorganize the industry. He believed less in industry than in some all-encompassing enterprise. In this he was a true son of Prussia—*Stockpreusse*—and a guide to Lenin. The future world, he insisted, would have to become "a single inseparable economic community." The nation-states did not fit into this eminently rational universe and Rathenau the patriot pronounced this cold truth in only a subdued way. The implication, of course, was German hegemony, in financial and industrial terms, over the European continent. There would be no need to make war if the logic of industry settled the matter peacefully and conclusively. Rathenau's idea of industry was not narrowly determined by the contemporary obsession with monopoly and profit, but was concerned with resource allocation and efficiency.

He sensed that the forces unleashed by modern industry, unless integrated through organizational networks and balances, would destroy each other. In 1912, when the British Imperial General Staff and the French Etat Major had already decided where to meet any future German offensive in northern France, and while Russia increased its mass armies, Lord Haldane had come to Berlin and then gone, without an agreement. Rathenau suggested caps on arms procurement, limitation of budgets, verification through an international court of accounts, and limitation of troop numbers according to population. In December 1913 he expanded on the politico-economic framework needed to move towards lasting peace:

> Trade legislation has to be made compatible, syndicates have to be compensated, customs revenue has to be divided and losses have to be made up. The aim is economic unity, equal, possibly superior, to that of the US. Within this system there would no longer be backward, stagnating or unproductive parts. Concomitantly nationalistic hatred would lose its edge ... If the European economy is fused, and this will happen sooner than we think, politics will also be fused. This is not global peace, not universal disarmament and certainly not the end of conflict. But it reduces rivalry, saves energies and makes for a civilization of common purpose.

But few in Europe listened. Rathenau's message was about a future still in the making. Europe was being driven on one side by vast optimism in economic terms, and on the other by deep pessimism in strategic terms. "Es ist nichts," Archduke Franz Ferdinand repeated while he was bleeding to death. "It is nothing." He had been shot by a Bosnian Serb, a member of a student terrorist group called Mlada Bosna (Young Bosnia), assisted by a Pan-Serb secret society called the Black Hand, sponsored in turn by the Serb secret service. The bullets were fired at the heir to the crowns of Austria and Hungary and his wife, at Sarajevo in Bosnia on June 28, 1914, and within less than six weeks led to the Great War. "The great seminal catastrophe of our century," to quote the US diplomat-cum-historian George F. Kennan, was to leave nothing unchanged: not the proud nation-states of Europe, not the relationship of the sexes, not poetry, painting or music, not the idea of the past or any vision of the future, not the human soul. To quote the title of the poet Robert Graves' memoir of the trenches, it was *Goodbye to All That*.

War had loomed for decades but never materialized, the chancelleries of Europe traditionally going to the brink, but not beyond. Self-preservation among the old elites played a role, as did the logic of industrial and financial interdependence and also the recognition that whatever could be gained in war would be nothing compared to what every nation was bound to lose the moment war broke out.

War seemed patently absurd, but it happened nevertheless, and events even showed logic and sequence—as well as chaos, incompetence and blindness. The Austrian generals, possessed by a combination of arrogance and anxiety, felt that only a short victorious war against Serbia could save the monarchy, while it carried with it the risk of a crushing Russian attack in the east. The Tsar, when signing the mobilization order setting the giant Russian army in motion, said, "It is the wish of the people." He knew that, if he did not sign, tsardom would be at risk from Pan-Slavist hysteria, while if he signed, only a miracle could save the Caesaro-Papism of the Romanovs. Jules Cambon, the French minister, knew that France, in order to save its alliances, would have to go to war, although direct French interests were not at stake in the Balkans. Bethmann Hollweg, the German Chancellor, sensed that, after the first moves, what followed was bound to be "a leap in the dark." The Kaiser, in spite of his boyish bragging, wanted to stop the westward thrust against France when suddenly faced with the prospect of war on two fronts. But His Majesty was advised by the chief of staff that, if he did so, he would no longer have an army but only a chaotic rabble.

The chain of events from the murder of the Archduke to the guns of August does indeed recall the lines that Leopold von Ranke, Graves' great uncle, had written about the march of human folly almost a century before:

> It is neither blindness nor ignorance that ruins nations and states. Not for long do they ignore where they are heading. But deep inside them is a force at work, favored by nature and reinforced through habit, that drives them forward irresistibly as long as there is still any energy in them. Divine is he who controls himself. Most humans recognize their ruin, but they carry on regardless.

Stefan Zweig, the distinguished Jewish Viennese writer, echoed Ranke when he described the start of war in his memoirs: "The issue was not the small border regions. I have no other explanation than this excess of power becoming the tragic consequence of that inner dynamism accumulated during those 40 years of power, driving towards a violent explosion."

Surely Austria had enough archdukes to replace the unhappy victim of Serb terror, and so be enabled to stumble on? The vast and heterogeneous empire could ill afford a war, major or minor, for fear of all its nationalities making their claims and overthrowing the precarious balances between Austrians and Hungarians, Protestants, Catholics and Orthodox, Christians and Jews; national aspirations meeting head-on the supranational elites of the monarchy, the bureaucracy, the military and the aristocracy. In Berlin, Archduke Franz Ferdinand had not been seen as a friend of the Dual Alliance. His loss was deemed to be "somehow tolerable," as a high official of the Wilhelmstrasse stated. But the assassination was indeed more than a cold-blooded, senseless murder. It was an attack on the Habsburg monarchy, to demonstrate its weakness. So, the reaction would have to offer proof of Austrian strength. Whatever Austrian diplomats and generals might decide, the German national interest was at stake, for the Danube monarchy was its last ally to count for anything—Italy was unlikely to stand up against the naval powers controlling the Mediterranean.

If the Austrians could administer a political humiliation to the regime in Belgrade, that was fine; even a surgical strike leading to Serb surrender was acceptable. "Now or never," William II remarked approvingly on the margins of a report from Vienna, "the Serbs must be put in their place." But if such strategies ran out of control and Russia marched against the central powers, it was at least preferable that the resulting war began with an Austrian move rather than a German one, as in the latter case the Austrians were unlikely to meet their treaty obligations. The possibilities for escalation were not ignored or excluded but only the first two steps were deliberately accepted. The rest had a kind of fatalistic quality. The situation was even made worse by the Schlieffen Plan, of whose details the Austrians had only a faint idea, which excluded the possibility of Germany attacking Russia first before turning to France, let alone restricting the war to eastern Europe. The Austrians were unaware that, given the westward thrust of the plan, they would have to face the Russian onslaught alone, without German reinforcements. And if Italy could not be bought off, the Austrian armies would face a desperate two-front war.

After the Sarajevo murder, the Russian secret police, the Ochrana, had spread the word that all Slavic brothers now had to stand together and fight. At the same time, the Wilhelmstrasse issued to the Austrians what became known as the "blank check"—the promise to stand behind the Austrians come what may. This was a dramatic departure from Bismarck's wisdom; now to encourage the Austrians to go ahead, and to do this in the knowledge of their sclerotic diplomatic machinery, meant that Germany's very existence was being put at risk for interests other than its own.

Meanwhile, the European diplomacy that had, only one year before, helped to settle the Balkan Wars of 1912–13 fell into a state of limbo. In the first phase, there was an absence of recognition that this time the crisis might escalate into the Great War. In the second phase, the vital strategic overview was obscured by the immediate tactical concern of how to preserve the cohesion of the two blocs facing each other, the central powers and the *Entente,* and to give reassurance to their weakest members, Austria and Russia. In the third phase, the Russian mobilization was moving at high speed.

The Germans were close to despair. They realized that Austrian diplomacy worked far too slowly to pre-empt Russian mobilization and effect a *fait accompli* against the despised Serb regime in Belgrade. But there was still hope, or so Bethmann Hollweg believed, that the Tsar might withdraw, that France would advise peace and that, as a consequence, the *Entente* would fall apart. Britain could have had a key role but, almost paralyzed at home by the prospect of civil war in Ireland, the Cabinet failed to act while there was still time. Ultimately, the war that followed was a self-fulfilling prophecy. Because all the powers believed, more or less, that the Great War was inevitable sooner or later, their efforts were directed much more at finding the right moment to strike and at preserving their alliances than at securing the peace. Thus the alliances, instead of preventing war, made it almost inevitable. Every single country had, ultimately, defensive motives masquerading behind offensive ones. Charles de Gaulle, at the time a young army officer, soon to be thrown into the bloody chaos of Verdun, thirty years later summed up what began. He called it "La guerre de trente ans de notre siècle," the twentieth century's Thirty Years War.

7

DANCE OF DEATH

Helmuth von Moltke had always warned his officers that no strategic plan would outlast the first encounter with the enemy. The truth of this was visited upon the German troops in August 1914, advancing in massive columns in the west, breaking through the fortifications of Liège on the Meuse river, to the north of Verdun, and heading, in a huge scythe movement, for Paris. By ignoring Belgium's neutrality—a "scrap of paper," Bethmann Hollweg remarked dismissively—Germany ensured the deployment of the British Expeditionary Force, for which the Schlieffen Plan did not allow. Neither did it allow for Liège holding out for ten rather than two days, for the Belgians immobilizing their railways, or for reservists in uncomfortable new boots not achieving the marching rates of the regulars. The Germans were also eight divisions short of the numbers posited by the Plan. The advancing troops got in each other's way, inexperienced field commanders made serious blunders, intelligence was muddled, the offensive was lacking in depth and the forward-deployed French divisions were defeated but not destroyed. When the first German mounted patrols arrived at the Marne river, taxis were ferrying the last reserves from Paris to the front. What the French soon celebrated as the *miracle de la Marne,* the Germans experienced as the failure of their grand strategy. The strategic initiative was lost forever; defense triumphed over attack. Artillery forced attackers and defenders alike into the trenches. There the enemy was not only the one on the other side of no man's land; it was also the rain, mud, vermin, cold, darkness, loneliness and despair.

In *Im Westen nichts Neues—All Quiet on the Western Front*—by Erich Maria Remarque, the protagonist is shot by an enemy sniper, on a quiet and otherwise unremarkable day. At the other end of the literary post-war spectrum, Ernst Jünger, a career infantry officer decorated with the Pour le Mérite, Prussia's highest award for gallantry under enemy fire, wrote *In Stahlgewittern—Storm of Steel*—trying to make sense of chaos and find heroism in the blood-soaked mud. From Ypres to the Chemin des Dames, from Verdun to the mountains of the Vosges, two winding systems of trenches were juxtaposed, the opposing troops often within earshot, the distance between the trenches not much more than a well-thrown hand grenade, snipers putting a deadly premium on every careless move.

In the west, the German grand strategy failed, as it did not yield the planned victory within six weeks, but in the east, the strategic defense worked better than expected. The Russian armies had to bypass the fortifications of Poznan, massively improved only during the last few years, to attack East Prussia. There they met units composed of local men fighting among vast marshes, lakes and waterways not so much for king and country as for farm and family. The Germans made use of their treacherous terrain to block, encircle and defeat the advancing Russians, who were vastly superior in numbers but inferior in technology and intelligence. Hundreds of thousands of Russians were taken prisoner, and Hindenburg and Ludendorff, his chief of staff, became national heroes. Farther south, the Russian armies were more successful, advancing in Galicia against the forces of the Austro-Hungarian Empire. The battle of Groddeck devoured tens of thousands from both sides. After a few months, war in the east also became static. Austrian regiments had to be bolstered by German reinforcements before they were able to withstand pressure or take back the initiative. The horrible losses in the east, the destructive impact of the war on a multinational empire and the fact that Germans and Austrians were forever unable to coordinate their grand strategy caused second thoughts in Vienna, leading to mutual distrust and a mood of impending doom.

In spite of all the blood and fortune spent, or more likely because of them, neither the *Entente* powers nor the central powers tried to limit the war, let alone sued for peace. Instead, every effort was made to widen the scope of weaponry used. Concentrated artillery and greatly increased numbers of machine guns, trench mortars, flame-throwers, poison gas and ultimately tanks were designed to break through enemy trenches, mostly in vain. Strategic widening of the war took place at sea. The German battle fleet, once the centerpiece of Germany's global aspirations, was reduced to lingering in port except for a few valiant singlehanded actions and the battle of Jutland. The Royal Navy was outgunned and left with a bloody nose, but the German fleet remained in harbor thereafter. Effort was transferred to submarine war. German U-boats attacked Allied shipping plying the North Atlantic and the Mediterranean very effectively until Lloyd George forced the Admiralty to adopt the convoy system.

The British naval blockade, way out in the Atlantic, cut off German supplies. But submarines firing their torpedoes from under water had difficulty identifying targets through their periscopes. When a German commander sank the British liner *Lusitania* with hundreds of Americans on board in 1915, it brought the United States closer to intervention on the *Entente* side. The German High Command was forced into a strategic gamble as unrestricted U-boat warfare would sooner or later bring the United States into the war. But in the spring of 1917 the German Admiralty, ignorant of North American industrial power and political resolve, promised victory and carried on regardless.

Most moving of guns and ammunition was still done by horses, but there was no more role for cavalry except in eastern Europe. Aircraft were used first to direct artillery fire against enemy positions, then to drop bombs. Inevitably, dogfights began, and young cavalry officers like Manfred von Richthofen—later the legendary "Red Baron" at the head of his "circus"—found a new and irresistible challenge in the air. But air power was never really integrated with ground action until August 1918.

A few months into the war, German industry had run out of its stocks of saltpeter. Without the Haber-Bosch process for producing nitrogen from the air, the production of ordnance would have ceased some time in 1915, and with it the war. The Allies were in no better shape, with British artillery on the Western Front reduced to an allowance of ten rounds a day in 1915 because of a shortage of shells from the factories. Walther Rathenau, formerly a vocal critic of the Kaiser's strategy, became the chief organizer of Germany's war industries.

Under the impact of war, Germany changed from a constitutional monarchy into a thinly disguised military dictatorship, with the Kaiser reduced to protocol functions and the Reichstag to rubber-stamping one bill after another for the issuing of war loans. The loans could only be redeemed if and when Germany finally won the war. On the western side, taxes were raised, but much of the financing of the war came from the United States. So the Allies, too, were caught in a debt trap. There were many reasons why the war went on as long as it did: the way it was financed on both sides played a large part. The Great War devoured all material resources, ruined civilian life, gave power to the military as never before, stifled public discourse, inflated the currency, expanded the public debt beyond any reasonable chance of repayment, mortgaged foreign holdings, killed small enterprises and effected an unprecedented economic dictatorship in the countries involved.

In Germany, politics fell silent, diplomacy was paralyzed and total mobilization produced its own momentum. Four hundred German university professors, most of them luminaries in their respective fields, launched a passionate indictment of the western powers for siding with Russian barbarism, and having no religion but materialism. Germany was seen as fighting a defensive war, having been encircled, and was now entitled to safeguard its interests throughout Europe by proclaiming strategic war aims. These had not driven the countries into war; rather war produced the war aims, giving itself a meaning that had been absent before, and by implication fueling the furore indefinitely, to the bitter end.

While the German war aims comprised placing eastern-central Europe under German domination and, in the west, annexation of the port of Antwerp and the iron ore deposits of Lorraine and Belgium, the western allies were no less ambitious in reserving for themselves large pieces of Germany. The nations making up the Danube monarchy were seen as potential allies, hence the propaganda that Austria-Hungary had to be destroyed. Russia, as well as seeking the final dismemberment of the Austro-Hungarian

Empire, wanted to secure the Dardanelles and demanded a stake in the Baltic approaches and much of Germany's Baltic coast. For all the nations engaged, this was to be the war to end all wars. But the means to achieve this noble end were mutually exclusive, and instead of ending the war they prolonged it until the final and complete exhaustion of one side. Instead of embarking on secret peace feelers and confidential negotiations, as had been diplomatic practice in earlier wars, both sides sent out their diplomats and bankers to help widen the theaters of war.

At first, the central powers scored a success when Turkey joined their side, fearing a Russian attack against the Dardanelles. Without German advice—in fact, massive German logistical support—the Turkish war effort would have ended before it really began, in breakdown and defeat. Instead, the Germans advised the Turkish commanders to fortify as quickly as possible the weakest spot in their defenses, the Gallipoli peninsula south of Istanbul, and at the same time to send a detachment across the Sinai to cut off the Suez Canal. This failed dismally, but at Gallipoli the Turkish troops, reinforced by German engineers, withstood the Allied invasion from the sea for more than ten months, throughout 1915, finally forcing the Allies to give up and evacuate the strategic peninsula.

The *Entente*, after having lost at Gallipoli, won in Rome, and in Tokyo—persuading the Japanese government that to win the German inheritance in the Far East was worth a declaration of war against Germany. But this was unimportant compared to Italy's entry into the war on the western side, which tipped the balance of forces. The Triple Alliance of Germany and Austria with Italy had always been an unlikely proposition in case of war against the Mediterranean sea power of Britain and France, who could also promise Adriatic islands and the southern provinces of Imperial Austria as a reward. On top of all this, a number of palms were greased and no questions asked. When Italy entered the war, the Austrians had to defend on two fronts, enabled to do so only by massive German help. Brusilov's offensive against the Austrians in June 1916, in which the Russians captured a quarter of a million men, finally persuaded Romania to join the *Entente*.

After three terrible winters, in early 1917 the war hung in the balance. Russia's February revolution brought a new elite to power who, however, made the fatal mistake of continuing the war. The German High Command, when approached by Lenin from his exile in Zurich, not only promised him and his entire entourage a safe passage through Germany; the generals also furnished the enemy's enemy with plenty of gold to carry out his nefarious designs and overthrow the Provisional Government, which had succeeded the Tsarist regime. Little did Germany's cunning soldiers know that they had entered into a pact with the Devil and that they, after the German workers' uprising that the Bolshevik leader was sure to foment, were next on Lenin's list.

Lenin's Bolshevik coup in St. Petersburg finally took Russia out of the war, after the Russian armies had fallen apart and the German troops had gone as far as they could without overstretching their supply lines. Lenin's logic was that, whatever the Germans might gain at the conference table at Brest-Litovsk, they would lose once the revolution cut the ground from under their feet. So on paper Germany was, once the peace treaty was signed, the master of eastern-central Europe, from the German border to Russia, with nothing but a chessboard of weak states to be overseen and directed from Berlin. Most important, the breakdown of Russia in the east allowed the German High Command to transport over one million soldiers to Flanders to secure victory in the west.

Things would not have looked bad for the central powers, had it not been for the looming American intervention. But the German High Command, like the Wilhelmstrasse, was inclined to underrate its impact. They still believed the Admiralty's bragging that most American troop ships would be sunk before they ever reached European waters. The High Command was confident of securing final victory through one last overpowering thrust before the Americans were able to deploy in any numbers. Instead of translating victory in the east into a realistic and timely peace offer to the western allies, the German leaders carried on regardless, victims of their own war aims, the war's finances and war propaganda.

Almost as potent as the fresh, well-fed and well-equipped American troops were the combined germs of nationalism and socialism broadcast by the Russian Revolution to the armies of the Austro-Hungarian Empire and into German industrial cities. Moreover, President Woodrow Wilson, a political science professor from Princeton University, knew that nothing less than a crusade and a world vision would do if he were to send American soldiers to die in Europe. That was the birth of the "Fourteen Points," also meant to be a democratic challenge to Lenin's communist vision and to limit the Allies' war aims in Europe, while at the same time holding out hope to the Germans that after the war there would be a future. Only to the overstretched empires of the Ottomans and the Habsburgs were the Fourteen Points a death sentence, since their constituent parts would become nation-states, following the principle of self-determination. Without the Germans—or, for that matter, the *Entente* powers—realizing, Lenin's battle cry and Wilson's vision had changed the overall nature of the war. The Great War of Europe had turned into world war, and the war of the nations into the war of ideologies.

Daily life in Germany had been transformed beyond recognition by the trials and tribulations of war. No one could remember so much cold, hunger and misery, and the great influenza epidemic of 1918 was to take away hundreds of thousands weakened through years of deprivation. Although prices were frozen, the currency was inflated and incomes lagged far behind in spite of nominal increases. Money had lost about two-thirds of its value and the public debt had risen to menacing proportions, while the middle classes had signed up for government bonds that, in the case of defeat, were unlikely ever to be redeemed. There was nothing to purchase anyway beyond the daily rations. Hunger drove the urban population to trade for food whatever could be traded—although sanctions were severe. Farmers hoarded whatever they could hide from the authorities. Exploitation and misery fueled social unrest, which from time to time flared up in strikes and demonstrations, in spite of the official ban. Class structures were crumbling in the cities much as in the countryside and women had been drafted to do men's work, the war inadvertently giving a cruel push to the cause of female emancipation. The standards of right and wrong were crumbling. The state was claiming treasure and blood in quantities that no tyrant of the past would ever have dared to extract.

In the early days of the war, *Burgfrieden,* harmony on the Home Front, had been pronounced in an effort to unite the German people behind their leaders and silence all doubt and criticism. Censorship of news and the self-censorship of parliament added to the leaden atmosphere. The hope was to utilize military victory as a surrogate for constitutional reform, and glory as a tonic for the nation. In 1916, when the military authorities tightened their control over production and consumption, a bargain was struck between the generals and the trade unions called *Vaterländisches Hilfsdienstgesetz* (Patriotic Support Bill). The military could from now on draft everybody, men and women, into production. Private ownership even of major companies became subject to military orders. The trade unions, in turn, were offered a massive say in the running of companies. Workers' councils (*Betriebsräte*) were set up, which as well as supervising matters of management had to be consulted on working conditions.

After the first Russian revolution in February 1917, the Kaiser announced the German equivalent of "a land fit for heroes," promising that once the war was won, there would be far-reaching constitutional reform and a revision of the three-class franchise in Prussia that ever since the constitution of 1849 made sure that voting power was organized according to the amount of direct tax paid. In mid-July 1917 the Reichstag seriously debated the worsening situation at the fronts for the first time, and even dared, though in closed session, to criticize the Admiralty's great gamble of unrestricted U-boat warfare, which risked American intervention. The issuing of new war bonds was made conditional on the government's accepting a "peace resolution" for a settlement "without annexations and reparations." Bethmann Hollweg, having lasted as Chancellor since 1909, was ousted, but the center-left majority now finding its voice was unable to produce from its own ranks a convincing leader, thus leaving the powers that be, the Military High Command, unchallenged.

It was the Western Front, however, not the Home Front, that collapsed first. Ludendorff's spring 1918 offensive drove the Allies back 40 miles and reached the Marne for the first time since 1914, but there were insufficient reserves of troops, supplies and means of transportation to consolidate and exploit the gains. Even with the advent, in early summer 1918, of many German divisions from the east at the Western Front, the overall correlation of forces was moving inexorably against the central powers. The massive offensives of the summer and autumn of 1918 threw more troops into the battle than ever before and at one stage they got within 40 miles of Paris. But the soldiers were worn out, hungry, badly equipped and shaken in their morale, and there was a sharp increase in the numbers of them surrendering.

The Germans had no weapons to fight the tanks that were suddenly making their appearance and breaking through lines thought to be impregnable. By 1918 the Allies had 800 of them—the Germans, twenty. The Americans appeared in large numbers and made their weapons felt. By the end of September, most German divisions, though still deep in enemy territory, were in a poor state. Bad news from the Austrian fronts added to the doom and gloom. It was time to begin the endgame while there was still a chance of a negotiated peace instead of one dictated by the victors to the vanquished. The long-term chances of equilibrium and stability throughout Europe hinged more on the ability of the German armies to hold the front line than on the enlightened statecraft of the *Entente* powers.

A government composed of the center-left in the Reichstag was formed, but even now it was under a Chancellor from a princely house, Max von Baden, who had no parliamentary experience and was in bad health. On paper, within weeks, Germany was transformed into a parliamentary monarchy on the Westminster model, with a strong dose of traditional federalism also incorporated. But all of this was too little, too late. The western allies simply failed to recognize that the German political scenery had changed decisively. Precious days and weeks were lost in October before the government in Berlin followed the orders of the High Command situated in Spa on the Belgian border, to sue for an armistice in order to save a negotiating position instead of facing wholesale breakdown.

8

A PEACE TO END ALL PEACE

The armistice was signed on November 11, 1918. But even before, mutiny had broken out in the German battle fleet, preventing it from sailing for the last bloody engagement that the Admiralty had planned, in order to go down with colors flying and guns blazing. The magic of military discipline was broken as armed sailors set up workers' and soldiers' councils, tore the insignia from their officers' uniforms and set out, mostly by train, to spread the word that the war was over and that revolution was the answer to all the suffering of the past. Within days there were the red flags of communism all over German cities, revolutionary councils formed and radical slogans displayed, all inspired by the Bolshevik revolution in Russia.

Was this a revolution? Yes and no: it was, as it turned out, above all the outcry of a nation that had suffered too much, that had lost its confidence in its leaders, that was physically exhausted and sunk in despair. It was not an attempt, carefully prepared, to create a new Germany, a new society or a new millennium. It was not even an attempt to take bloody revenge for all the futile suffering of the last four years, but rather the breakdown of a worn-out nation, its gods fallen, its ideals shattered, its self-respect broken. The war had destroyed not only the future, but also the past. The chiefs of the General Staff had told the Kaiser that only a hero's death in battle would offer a chance to save the Hohenzollern dynasty. True or not, William II preferred a comfortable train ride to neutral Holland where the government had offered him exile. Arriving at the Dutch border, his first request was for a good cup of

English tea. The disaster that he had helped to bring about he left behind without wasting a second glance. The memoirs he set out to write were of utter banality. The German drama had long bypassed him.

The General Staff tried to organize the orderly retreat of millions of German soldiers from Russia, Ukraine, northern Italy, France and Belgium. The government in Berlin had all but lost control. Reich-Chancellor Prince Max von Baden was happy to formally transfer power—or what was left of it—into the hands of Friedrich Ebert, leader of the social democrats in the Reichstag, a trade unionist and a man of order. When the Prince told him that the fate of the Reich now rested in his hands, Ebert replied that he had lost two sons for Germany. But it was by no means clear who would emerge in control, out of the chaos arising from the absence of duly constituted authority. A race ensued between communists and social democrats to proclaim the German Republic: Karl Liebknecht inaugurated the socialist republic from the balcony of the Hohenzollerns' town palace, while social democrat Philipp Scheidemann replied in the Reichstag by stating that parliamentary democracy was dawning. Liebknecht was a communist firebrand, Scheidemann a middle-of-the-road working class leader. These symbolic acts merely outlined the ideological rifts that were now to embroil the entire country in civil war, except in the west where Allied troops made their appearance, welcomed by the middle classes, who tended to prefer enemy order to German disorder.

Ebert immediately established the Council of People's Deputies. While its name sounded revolutionary enough, the six members were moderate socialists and social democrats. The country thus had a transitional source of authority until elections were held and the resulting national assembly could create a new constitutional order. The General Staff in Kassel, now led by Hindenburg's new quartermaster-general Wilhelm Groener, needed democratic authority; the Berlin-based Council of People's Deputies needed effective military power for the civil war that was about to be initiated by the Spartakus group. The latter soon transformed itself into Germany's Communist Party, and relied for its successes on revolutionary soldiers and their weapons, on the radical opposition to the trade union establishment, support from Soviet Russia and the general state of exhaustion throughout the country.

Four factors helped the transition from empire to republic and the avoidance of communism. First of all, the trade union leaders were united with Ebert and his military allies in rejecting all attempts at Bolshevik revolution. Second, the employers and the trade unions, building on their wartime alliance, established the Zentralarbeitsgemeinschaft—Central Working Committee—and together they did all in their power to transform the revolutionary upheaval into a movement for higher wages and better working conditions. The eight-hour working day was established, workers' councils were confirmed and a minimum wage was introduced, although it was soon made meaningless by the eroding effects of inflation. Third, the generals forged a *quid pro quo* with Ebert and the People's Deputies in Berlin, securing their own authority while offering, in turn, security to the politicians. All this meant that no expropriations of big companies or landed estates would take place, while the immediate demands of blue-collar workers would be met. Finally, it helped that the western allies refused to negotiate with any authority other than the Ebert–Groener axis between Berlin and Kassel: the victors needed an authority in Germany to sign the peace terms to be decided by the Paris peace conference.

The triangle of authority laid out between the Berlin authorities, the Supreme Command in Kassel and the holders of industrial power wanted to bring home the soldiers, turn industry back to peacetime production, negotiate a peace and create a parliamentary republic. While street fighting was going on in Berlin the elections of January 19, 1919 gave a three-quarters majority to the parties of the center-left: the Social Democrats, the leftwing liberal Deutsche Demokratische Partei and the old Catholic Center Party. The old National Liberal Party reemerged under Gustav Stresemann, adopting the name of Deutsche Volkspartei, and so did the Deutschkonservative Partei, now under the name of Deutschnationale Volkspartei. The Communists had rejected the elections as just another bourgeois plot, while the radical Volkische fringe on the right was conspicuous by its absence.

As fighting continued in Berlin, a safe venue had to be found for the German National Assembly. Weimar was chosen not because of its associations with Goethe and Schiller, but because the little town in Thuringia offered relative calm, a suitable building in its National Theater, enough to eat and, above all, security against a Leninist coup. In fact, for the duration of the constitutional deliberations, Weimar was guarded by the Freikorps Maercker, one of the many freelance military units in search of employment.

Germans looked to Weimar to open a new chapter of national history. Nine out of ten had no stomach for Leninist revolution, but eight out of ten were ready to give democracy a try, to attempt to learn from the victors. Constitution making in Weimar was, of course, coupled to peace making in Paris. While the Germans tried to take their fate into their own hands, it was all too evident that it was to be decided, first and foremost, at the Paris conference tables.

In the next few months, the communist uprisings were suppressed in Berlin and elsewhere. Karl Liebknecht and Rosa Luxemburg were shot in the course of a mopping-up operation by Freikorps troops in the service of the government, giving rise to a martyrs' myth. The Munich *Räterepublik* ended with its leader, Kurt Eisner's assassination, then the killing of hostages, mostly elderly professors from the Art Academy, by the revolutionaries. This was followed by bloody revenge on the part of the Freikorps and volunteers moving in from the mountains of Upper Bavaria, some of them under the swastika. The rest was left to the courts, which meted out draconian punishment, death sentences included.

The men and women assembled in the celebrated National Theater in the heart of the city of Weimar were aware of what was at stake. They wanted a perfect constitution, taking the best from the German tradition and adding what they found convenient from the west. The German past offered a strong bureaucracy and administrative courts, one man, one vote elections and a legislative role for parliament. Federalism too had survived war and revolution, and while it proved impossible to reduce the old imbalance inherent in the overwhelming size and weight of the state of Prussia, for the first time now the Reich had power over direct taxation, which was soon to give rise to sweeping legislation. The trade unions saw to it that the elements of state socialism and the achievements of recent months were preserved in constitutional form. The middle classes secured guarantees of individual property. The social democrats tried to keep the door open for more socialism, once they achieved an overall majority—something they regarded as merely a matter of time thanks to the internal contradictions of capitalism.

Restoration of the monarchy was not seriously debated because even the conservatives-turned-nationalists would have been hard pressed to name a likely candidate. Instead, the left-wing liberals inspired by Max Weber, the famous sociologist, and Friedrich Naumann, the Nationalsozial leader, created an Ersatzkaiser and guardian of the constitution in the shape of the new office of Reich President. This was done not out of theoretical considerations, but primarily to create a rock on which all anti-republican movements of the future should founder. But there was also a belief in the benefits of personal authority and the hope that a popularly elected chief executive would forever block socialist experiments. Ebert, however, had forebodings of crises to come and, although a dyed-in-the-wool social democrat and now himself Reich President, he regretted the bonds of tradition and legitimacy that had been broken with the fall of the monarchy. His fellow social democrats, for their part, insisted on installing a system for referendums, assuming that this would provide a means to overrule middle-class majorities in parliament.

So, while parliament passed legislation and voted governments into or out of power, both the President and the popular referendum curtailed parliamentary primacy. The eagle remained Germany's state symbol, but one could say that now it had three heads ready to fight each other. On the face of it, the constitution looked like a piece of perfect locksmithing. In reality, it would open the gates to the barbarians once the democratic honeymoon was over.

Meanwhile in Paris, twenty-seven states were invited to attend the conference to make peace, many of them still in the process of defining themselves, forming a government and fighting their neighbors, many of their leaders at best inexperienced, at worst bent on expansion. The vanquished states were not invited: Germany, Austria, Hungary, Turkey, Bulgaria. The Russia of the Tsars had been sent a formal invitation, but there was no one to accept. Thus, Germany and Russia, the two most powerful nations on the European continent, were conspicuous by their absence. The conference was conceived as an open forum, and since the Supreme Council, composed of the United States, Britain, France, Italy and Japan, never managed to agree upon an overall organizing principle, it got lost in detail, wishful thinking and huge contradictions. Prominent among them was the incompatibility of Wilson's high-flying idealism with French paranoia.

Wilson wanted to call a new world into being based on national self-determination, democracy and free trade, the absence of secret diplomacy and a League of Nations to ensure peace. He understood neither the role of the old empires nor the conglomerate nature of most of the new nation-states, in particular Czechoslovakia, Poland and Yugoslavia. Nor did he realize that, for the post-war order to work, it needed an open-ended American commitment to put right every wrong and be the world's policeman.

French leaders, by contrast, were obsessed with carving up Germany, extracting vast reparations and building a *petite entente* of Czechoslovakia, Yugoslavia and Romania around Germany in the east that would also serve to contain the Bolshevik revolution. They were painfully aware that without *les Anglosaxons* the balance of Europe, sooner or later, would be in the hands of Germany. Clemenceau, "le tigre," put up a desperate fight to achieve the permanent suppression of German power while knowing that, without British and American support, this was nothing but a dangerous delusion. Given the popular passions created by the war as well as the huge debt incurred by all the belligerent nations, there was no way to transcend the bitterness and co-opt the new German republic as a partner into the post-war system. By treating Germany as the arch-enemy and even propounding, in article 231 of the Versailles treaty, the sole responsibility of Germany for the outbreak of the war—a question that has since claimed vast stretches of library shelving—a self-fulfilling prophecy was created. This war-guilt clause was a newcomer in the diplomatic toolbox, used to extract huge reparations irrespective of the fact that, with Europe's biggest economy in permanent financial ruin, the world economy could not recover. Hence John Maynard Keynes, economic adviser to the British delegation, saying that this peace contained the seeds of the next war.

The other provisions of the treaty left Germany largely intact, but humiliated the country and created an all-encompassing resentment against the "dismal diktat" of Versailles. One-seventh of Germany's territory was cut off, Alsace and Lorraine in the west, and the western part of Poland in the east, giving the Polish republic access to the Baltic. In Upper Silesia and in Schleswig-Holstein, large chunks of territory were given to Poland and Denmark, respectively. The army had to be cut down to 100,000 regulars, while the battle fleet had to be handed over to the British, together with large parts of the merchant marine. Reparations in kind were to go to the areas of France and

Belgium devastated by the war. The Kaiser, now safe in Holland, was to be tried as a war criminal.

Paris in 1919 was not Vienna in 1815. The European system now created rested on the permanent exclusion of the two dominant powers on the Continent, Germany and Russia, and it even put a premium on their making common cause to unhinge the system. The Russians' fear of the capitalist world ganging up would give them a strong incentive to find a partner, and Poland, re-created from the lost lands of the Tsar and Kaiser, would serve as a catalyst for their union. The peacemakers in Paris did not realize that, in geostrategic terms, Germany was stronger after the war than before, since for the first time in thirty years France had no substantial ally in the east to contain German energy. Britain would concentrate on its empire, by now larger, but also more brittle than ever.

This peace was "a fragile compromise between American utopianism and European paranoia," said Henry Kissinger, with Germany in the center, dismembered but not destroyed. By the summer of 1919 it appeared that Germany had been defined, from inside and from outside, for a long time to come. On closer inspection it was evident, however, that only the first act in the great European drama had ended and that the curtain would soon rise again. What the script would be for the next act was as yet unknown. But the fringe groups and desperados of the radical left and right, traumatized by the birth pangs of the Weimar Republic, were certainly ready to strike as soon as there was the chance to overthrow it.

EPILOGUE

Four months after the fall of the Berlin Wall in 1989 Margaret Thatcher convoked a colloquium of learned historians from Great Britain and the United States and put to them the question: "Have the Germans changed?" In the defining moment after the end of the Cold War Mrs. Thatcher wanted to know where Germany was going and, by implication, how Europe would be affected. The questions revealed deep-seated anxieties about Germany's past as much as about her present and future.

After the reunification of East and West, the German parliament decided in 1991 to honor old pledges and move the seat of government back to Berlin, the capital of Germany from 1871 to 1945. No one could be sure what effect this move would have on the style and substance of German politics. It was a shift from the provincial city of Bonn in the west, to Berlin in the east: Bonn is close to Benelux and the French border and Berlin is a only one hour by train from Poland. History was on the move again and Germany was possibly, Britain suspected, planning some kind of repeat performance: there seemed to be contemporary echoes in these concerns of Benjamin Disraeli's forebodings in 1871 about the "German revolution" and its effects on British interests. The same fears of a "German revolution" came quickly flooding back, in Germany as well as in Great Britain and the rest of Europe.

Berlin has a collection of buildings with resonances far beyond their immediate presence. The Reichstag on the edge of Berlin's old political square mile is an apt metaphor for the fusing of the past and the present. Some might consider it also to serve as a symbol of reassurance for Lady Thatcher, since it was a British architect, Sir Norman Foster, who gave the building its present shape. Leaving aside the bizarre fact that a new German political correctness would like to do away with its old name which supposedly smacks of empire and imperialism, the building with its powerful and massive Wilhelmine Renaissance structure and its transparent, ultramodern glass cupola, represents very well Germany's aspirations, past and present. During the last two decades of imperial Germany the Reichstag was the seat of an unruly parliament and the political focus of the ill-fated Weimar Republic. In early 1933 it was burnt down by a Communist arsonist who it is now believed was induced to do so by the Nazis, and in the years of Hitler's dictatorship it stood as an empty shell. In the last days of World War II it became the center of hand-to-hand fighting between the Red Army and desperate Wehrmacht troops. Some traces of machine-gun fire can still be seen today as well as the graffiti that Soviet soldiers left behind in the basement.

The neoclassical Brandenburg Gate, erected just before the French Revolution, has witnessed events from Napoleon's triumphant entry in 1806 to the victorious return of the Prussian guards from Paris in 1871; from the bitterness of civil war in 1918–19 to the torchlight parade of Hitler's storm troopers on the evening of January 30, 1933; from the blockade of Berlin by Stalin in 1948–49 to the building and dismantling of the wall in 1961 and 1989 respectively. A few yards south of the gate is a space where in 1938–9 Albert Speer, Hitler's legendary architect, built in record time the vast Neue Reichskanzlerei for the Führer. In 1945 a marble monument of the same stone was erected nearby, complete with vintage Soviet guns and tanks, to commemorate the victories of the Red Army between 1941 and 1945—there is no mention of course of their collaboration with Hitler and his henchmen two years previously. The same stone was used to build the Soviet embassy, the seat of Stalin's proconsul in central Europe which is today post-Soviet Russia's embassy. To the west of the gate extend many miles of a route used for centuries by traders and armies, interrupted only by the "siegessäule," a column celebrating Prussia's victory over France in 1871. Crowned by a gilt bronze goddess of victory, the column is adorned with gun barrels in a celebration of military triumph. To the east is the old promenade, "Unter den Linden," which once led to the splendid baroque Town Palace, built for the first Prussian king. Demolished in 1952 by the East German regime, it became an empty space where the proletariat assembled from time to time to thank its leaders for their existence.

In a landscape saturated with history and littered with monuments to human folly, the five decades of the Bismarckian empire stand out, for better and for worse, as the formative period of modern Germany. The nation-state which he created in 1871, notwithstanding European integration and economic globalization, is still the mold of political life. German corporatism, that perennial intimacy between big business and big finance, is only slowly opening up to the challenges of the world economy. The welfare state is still the fortress of social equilibrium and state control. Federalism of the age-old German type, entrenched in sixteen *land* capitals from Hamburg to Munich, is far from being a spent force in the Europe of Brussels. Of the many chapters of history none has formed and transformed Germany more deeply than the one that began at Versailles and was to end, forty-eight years later, at Versailles. Much as the Germans may have changed, Germany continues to be at the center of the ongoing drama of European history.

KEY FIGURES

Adenauer, Konrad (1876–1967). Son of Prussian non-commissioned officer, studied law, married into patrician family in Cologne, Mayor of Cologne 1917–33. First Chancellor of Federal Republic of Germany, *pater patriae*.

Ballin, Albert (1857–1918). German industrialist from Jewish family, turned Hamburg-America line into biggest shipping company of pre-1914 world. Advised the Kaiser against building battle fleet.

Bebel, August (1840–1913). Son of Prussian non-commissioned officer, became a turner and set up successful business. Leader of Social Democratic Party, called "the workers' Bismarck."

Berlepsch, Hans Baron von (1843–1926). High civil servant in Prussia, led negotiations with striking miners in 1889, subsequently Prussian Minister of Commerce.

Bernstein, Eduard (1850–1932). Social democratic politician of Jewish background. Although favored by Marx and Engels, he became the leading spirit of reformism.

Bethmann Hollweg, Theobald von (1856–1921). High civil servant, Chancellor 1909–17. A Hamlet character whose insights about the nature of William II's rule and the likely effect of war far exceeded his willingness to act.

Bismarck, Otto Prince (after 1871) von (1815–98). Conservative firebrand from Junker stock, expert in anti-revolutionary nation building. "Iron Chancellor" driven by *cauchemar des coalitions*. 3 vols of worthwhile memoirs.

Bülow, Bernhard von (1849–1929). Prince 1905, Foreign Secretary, Chancellor 1900–9. His vanity conspicuously exceeded his capacities. Reintroduced protectionist tariffs, supported battle fleet. 4 vols of bragging memoirs.

Caprivi, Leo von (1831–99). Count 1891, infantry general in charge of Reich Naval Office, successor to Bismarck as Chancellor 1890–94. Favored *détente* with Russia and informal alliance with Britain, was hated by agricultural lobby and nationalists. Unfairly overlooked.

Clemenceau, Georges (1841–1929). Radical French politician, called "le tigre," who would never forgive Germany for annexation of Alsace-Lorraine. Prime Minister 1917–20, determined hopeless French strategy at Paris peace conference.

Conrad von Hötzendorf, Franz (1852–1925). Austrian Chief of Staff 1906–11, 1912–17), chiefly responsible for aggressive Austro-Hungarian strategy in the Balkans 1908 and 1914. Instead of saving the monarchy through military triumph, he led it to ruin.

Disraeli, Benjamin, (after 1876) Lord Beaconsfield (1804–81). Tory leader, warned against "German revolution" in 1871, as British Prime Minister cooperated with Bismarck at Berlin Congress 1878 to prevent war with Russia.

Ebert, Friedrich (1871–1925). Social Democratic leader, in 1918 head of provisional government, forged alliance with Military High Command, first President of Weimar Republic.

Eisner, Kurt (1867–1919). Socialist leader in Bavaria, proclaimed republic on November 7, 1918, murdered on February 21, 1919 in Munich.

Franz Ferdinand (1863–1914). Archduke of Austria and successor to all the Habsburg crowns. Reform-minded, reorganized land and naval forces, married for love, murdered by Bosnian Serb on June 28, 1914 in Sarajevo with his wife.

Franz Joseph I (1830–1916). Emperor of Austria and King of Hungary. Presided over decline and fall of the Habsburg Empire. A bureaucrat, no vision, old school.

Frederick III (1831–88). German Emperor for 99 days, died of cancer. Married to Vicky, Princess Royal. Reform-minded. Took with him the hopes of liberal Germany.

Gambetta, Leon (1838–82). French politician, favored a radical republic. Escaped from encircled Paris in 1870 to organize war *à l'outrance* against German armies. But the moderates wanted peace and he had to resign.

Gaulle, Charles de (1890–1969). French army officer and statesman. After education at St. Cyr, served in 33rd Regiment under Pétain, taken prisoner at Verdun. Lifelong love-hate relationship with Germany.

Grey, Sir Edward (1862–1933). British Foreign Secretary 1905–16, turned *Entente Cordiale* with France into anti-German alliance and forced accession of Russia in 1907 against massive doubts in Liberal Party.

Haldane, Richard Burdon (1856–1928). Viscount 1911, British Secretary for War, impressed by Prussian army, reformed British forces after Boer War. Went to Berlin to achieve naval arms control in 1912.

Hindenburg, Paul von (1847–1934). Prussian field marshal. After defeating Russian armies in 1914 became popular hero and Germany's war leader 1916–18. Helped Hitler into power in 1933.

Hitler, Adolf (1889–1945). Son of minor Austrian official, formed by pre-1914 Vienna gutter milieu, volunteered to serve in Bavarian regiment, badly wounded at Western Front, decided to become politician. Totalitarian leader and "incarnation of evil" (Hans Bernd von Haeften).

Hohenlohe-Schillingsfürst, Chlodwig Prince (1819–1901). From south German grand family, as Chancellor he failed to leave any mark on politics except allowing William II to unfold his *persönliches Regiment.*

Joffre, Joseph (1852–1931). Maréchal de France, as member of Supreme Defense Council he was responsible for mobilization. Chiefly responsible for the *miracle de la Marne* in September 1914, member of Académie française 1918.

Katkov, Michael Nikiforowitsch (1818–87). Influenced by Hegel and impressed by British political system, in mid-life he became vocal spokesman for Tsarist absolutism based no longer on divine right but on radical Pan-Slavism. Sleepless workaholic.

Krupp, Friedrich (1812–87). Industrialist in Essen, the "king of the guns." Rose from small foundry business to commanding heights of German heavy industry. His "Villa Hügel," overlooking the Ruhr valley, of imperial dimensions.

Legien, Carl (1861–1920). German trade unionist. After fall of Bismarck's anti-socialist legislation, Legien accepted government offer to bring workers into political system. Interlocutor of Military High Command during World War I and promoter of political compromise in 1918–19.

Lenin, Wladimir Iljitsch (1870–1924). Russian revolutionary, helped by German High Command to overthrow Tsarist regime weakened by war. Proclaimed world peace through world revolution. Ordered Trotsky to sign Treaty of Brest-Litovsk as a mere prelude to Germany's social revolution.

Liebknecht, Karl (1871–1919). German socialist leader and, with Rosa Luxemburg, founder of Communist Party of Germany 1918. Shot by Freikorps troops.

Ludendorff, Erich (1865–1937). German military leader in World War I, single-minded militarist, wanted to force decision at Eastern Front, broke off Verdun strategy of "bleeding France white." In all but name, military dictator 1916–18.

Ludwig II (1845–86). King of Bavaria. Fanciful character, sponsored Richard Wagner, incurred huge debt through building his fantasies, was bribed by Bismarck into offering imperial rank to King of Prussia, became more and more mentally deranged.

Luxemburg, Rosa (1870–1919). Leading light among Marxist thinkers, militant German socialist and sensuous woman. Came from Jewish stetl in Russia, studied economics in Zurich. Organizer of Spartakus group and co-founder of Communist Party. Murdered by Freikorps troops in Berlin.

Max, Prince of Baden (1867–1929). Last Chancellor of Bismarckian Empire, liberal successor to the Grand Ducal crown of Baden. Appointed Chancellor October 3, 1918 to sue for peace. Transformed constitution, pronounced abdication of William II.

Moltke, Helmuth von (1800–91). Count 1870, Prussian field marshal, a legend in his time, integrated modern technology into warfare and won three wars (1864–71).

Napoleon III (1808–73). Empereur des Français 1852–70. After *coup d'état* forged a synthesis of authoritarian government and popular base. Sponsor of Italian nationalism, but opposed Prussian unification of Germany. Imprisoned at Sedan.

Nicolas II (1868–1918). Tsar of all the Russians. Wanted to continue autocracy, but was the weakest of all Russian rulers. Stumbled into Great War. Murdered by Bolsheviks.

Pétain, Philippe (1856–1951). Maréchal de France, an independent mind before 1914, Germany became his destiny. Successful commander 1914–18, restored morale among the shattered French troops, won great prestige. President of Vichy France 1940–45.

Rathenau, Walther (1867–1922). One of the most powerful industrialists of his time and a prolific writer, a Jewish outsider to the Jewish cause and a German outsider to the German cause. Organized German economic war effort and became Foreign Minister of Weimar Republic. Assassinated in 1922.

Scheidemann, Philipp (1865–1939). Socialist leader, proclaimed republic November 9, 1918 from window of Reichstag. One of 6 "people's commissars," appointed Ministerpräsident by Ebert in February 1919, resigned over Versailles Treaty.

Schlieffen, Alfred Count von (1833–1913). Chief of Prussian General Staff 1891–1905. The grand strategy named after him was a vast gamble, turning war on two fronts from a possibility to be avoided at all costs into an inevitable predicament.

Stresemann, Gustav (1878–1929). Liberal leader and Foreign Minister of Weimar Republic from 1923. From modest background, ambitious and energetic, confidant of the Military High Command, distrusted in Reichstag, described himself as

Vernunftrepublikaner, i.e., a Republican not through emotion but through reason.

Thiers, Adolphe (1797–1877). Moderate French politician under July monarchy. In opposition to Napoleon III. Opposed war against Germany, feared social revolution if war could not be stopped, negotiated peace with Bismarck 1871.

Tirpitz, Alfred (1849–1930). Ennobled 1900, naval officer, overambitious, energetic and able, designed grand strategy against Britain and planned battle fleet accordingly. A single-minded military man, he failed to grasp the fatal implications.

William I (1797–1888). King of Prussia, proclaimed German Emperor in 1871. A military man throughout his life; no Dr. Faustus, he found his Mephisto in Bismarck. Utterly unpopular as a diehard in 1848, he became the incarnation of the "good old days" once they were past.

William II (1859–1941). King of Prussia and German Emperor. "A most brilliant failure," his uncle Edward VII called him. Highly talented and utterly superficial, he wanted to create a kind of charismatic rule based on imperial glory and material well-being. He not only misread industrial Germany, but also found himself caught in a military confrontation that he had never anticipated. His afterlife in exile showed only unlimited banality of thought and action.

Wilson, Woodrow (1856–1924). 28th US President. Led USA into World War I, wanted to give direction and meaning to war effort through "Fourteen Points," but failed to impose his idealism on the European politicians assembled at the peace conference in 1919. At home, Congress refused to foot the bill and allow the United States to be drawn into precisely those entangling alliances that George Washington had advised against and that had cost so many lives during the war.

BIBLIOGRAPHY

ABRAMS, L. *Worker's Culture in Imperial Germany.* London, 1991.

ALBRECHT-CARRIE, R. *A Diplomatic History of Europe Since the Congress of Vienna.* London, 1958.

BALFOUR, M. *The Kaiser and His Times.* London, 1964.

BERGHAHN, W. *Imperial Germany, 1871–1914.* Oxford, 1994.

BLACKBOURN, D. *Class, Religion and Local Politics in Wilhelmine Germany.* London, 1981.

———. *The Long Nineteenth Century—A History of Germany, 1780–1918.* New York/Oxford, 1998.

BLACKBOURN, D., and G. ELEY. *The Peculiarities of German History: Bourgeois Society and Politics in Nineteenth-Century Germany.* Oxford, 1984.

BROSE, E. D. *German History, 1789–1871: From the Holy Roman Empire to the Bismarckian Reich.* Providence, 1997.

CECIL, L. *The German Diplomatic Service, 1871–1914.* Princeton, NJ, 1979.

———. *Wilhelm II: Emperor and Exile, 1900–1941.* Chapel Hill, NC, 1996.

CHAPPLE, G. ET AL. *The Turn of the Century: German Literature and Art, 1890–1915* (Modern German Studies, vol. V). Bonn, 1981.

CHICKERING, R. *Imperial Germany and a World Without War.* Princeton, NJ, 1975.

CRAIG, G. A. *Germany, 1866–1945* (Oxford History of Modern Europe). Oxford, 1978.

———. *Theodor Fontane: Literature and History in the Bismarck Reich.* Oxford, 1997.

———. *The Politics of the Prussian Army, 1640–1945.* Oxford, 1955.

ELEY, G. *Reshaping the German Right: Radical Nationalism and Political Change after Bismarck.* New Haven/London, 1980.

EVANS, R. J. (ED.). *Society and Politics in Wilhelmine Germany.* London, 1978.

EYCK, E. *Bismarck and the German Empire.* New York, 1958/London, 1950–58. (*Bismarck und das deutsche Reich.* München, 1978.)

FELDMANN, G. D. *Army, Industry, and Labor in Germany, 1914–1918.* Princeton, NJ, 1966.

FISCHER, F. *From Kaiserreich to the Third Reich: Elements of Continuity in German History, 1871–1945.* New York, 1967.

FRIEDRICH, O. *Blood and Iron: From Bismarck to Hitler. The von Moltke Family's Impact on German History.* New York, 1995.

GALL, L. *Bismarck: The White Revolutionary.* 2 vols, 1871–1898. Princeton, NJ, 1986. (*Bismarck: der weiße Revolutionär.* Frankfurt am Main, 1980.)

GEISS, I. *German Foreign Policy, 1871–1914.* London, 1976.

GUTTSMAN, W. L. *The German Social Democratic Party, 1875–1933.* London, 1987.

HENDERSON, W. O. *The Rise of German Industrial Power, 1834–1914.* London, 1975.

HOBSBAWM, E. J. *The Age of Empire, 1874–1914.* London, 1987.

HUNTINGTON, S. P. *The Clash of Civilizations and the Remaking of World Order.* New York, 1996.

JARAUSCH, K. H. *Students, Society and Politics in Imperial Germany: The Rise of Academic Illiberalism.* New York, 1985.

———. *The Enigmatic Chancellor Bethmann Hollweg and the Hubris of Imperial Germany.* New Haven, 1973.

KELLY, A. (ED.). *The German Worker.* Berkeley, 1987.

KENNAN, G. F. *The Decline of Bismarck's European Order: Franco-Russian Relations, 1875–1890.* Princeton, NJ, 1979.

KENNEDY, P. M. (ED.). *The War Plans of the Great Powers, 1880–1914.* London, 1979.

———. *The Rise and Fall of the Great Powers: Economic Change and Military Conflict from 1500 to 2000.* London, 1988.

KENT, G. *Bismarck and His Times.* Carbondale, 1978.

KESSLER, HARRY GRAF *Walther Rathenau: His Life and Work.* New York, 1930. (*Walther Rathenau: Sein Leben und Sein Werk.* Berlin-Grunewald, 1928.)

KISSINGER, H. A. *A World Restored: Metternich, Castlereagh and the Problems of Peace, 1812–1822.* New York, 1962.

———. *Diplomacy.* New York, 1994.

LAMBI, I. N. *Free Trade and Protection in Germany, 1868–1879.* (*Vierteljahrschrift für Sozial- und Wirtschaftsgeschichte/Beihefte* 44). Wiesbaden, 1963.

———. *The Navy and German Power Politics, 1862–1914.* Boston, 1984.

LANDES, D. S. *The Unbound Prometheus: Technological Change and Industrial Development in Western Europe from 1750 to the Present.* Cambridge, 1969.

———. *The Wealth and Poverty of Nations. Why Some Are So Rich and Some So Poor.* New York, 1998.

LERMAN, K. A. *The Chancellor as Courtier: Bernhard von Bülow and the Governance of Germany, 1900–1909.* Cambridge, 1990.

MILWARD, A. ET AL. *The Economic Development of Continental Europe, 1780–1870.* London, 1973.

MORISON, S. *Otto von Bismarck and Imperial Germany: A Historical Assessment.* Lexington, 1993.

NICHOLS, J. A. *Germany After Bismarck: The Caprivi Era, 1890–1894.* Cambridge, 1958.

ORLOW, D. *A History of Modern Germany, 1871 to Present.* Englewood Cliffs, 1987.

PFLANZE, O. *Bismarck and the Development of Germany.* 3 vols. Princeton, NJ, 1990.

———. *The Unification of Germany, 1848–1871* (European Problems Studies). Princeton, NJ, 1963.

RETALLACK, J. N. *Notables of the Right. The Conservative Party and Political Mobilization in Germany, 1876–1918.* Boston, 1988.

———. *Germany in the Age of Kaiser Wilhelm II.* Boston, 1996.

RICHIE, A. *Faust's Metropolis: A History of Berlin.* New York, 1998.

RÖHL, J. C. G. *The Kaiser and His Court: Wilhelm II and the Government of Germany.* New York, 1964.

ROSENBERG, A. *Imperial Germany: The Birth of the German Republic, 1871–1918.* Boston, 1964. (*Die Entstehung der Deutschen Republik 1871–1918.* Berlin 1928.)

ROSS, R. *Failure of Bismarck's Kulturkampf: Catholicism and State Power.* Washington, DC, 1998.

SACKETT, R. E. *Popular Entertainment, Class and Politics in Munich, 1900–1923.* Harvard, 1982.

SCHULZE, H. *Course of German Nationalism: From Frederick the Great to Bismarck.* Cambridge, 1991.

SHEEHAN, J. J. *German History, 1770–1866.* Oxford, 1981.

SHEEHAN, J. J. (ED.). *Imperial Germany.* New York/London, 1976.

SMITH, W. D. *European Imperialism in the Nineteenth and Twentieth Centuries.* New York/Oxford, 1982.

————. *Politics and the Sciences of Culture in Germany, 1840–1920.* New York/Oxford, 1991.

STERN, F. *Gold and Iron: Bismarck, Bleichröder and the Building of the German Empire.* London, 1977.

STEVENSON, D. *French War Aims Against Germany, 1914–1919.* New York, 1982.

STRANDMANN, H. Pogge-von (ED.). *Walter Rathenau: Industrialist, Banker, Intellectual and Politician: Notes and Diaries, 1907–1922.* Oxford, 1985. (*Rathenau, Walther: Tagebuch 1907–1922. Hrsg. u. kommentiert von Hartmut Pogge-von Strandmann.* Düsseldorf, 1967.)

STÜRMER, M. *The German Century.* London, 1999. (*Das Jahrhundert der Deutschen.* München, 1999.)

STÜRMER, M. ET AL. *Striking the Balance: Sal. Oppenheim Jr. & Cie. A Family and a Bank.* London, 1994. (*Wägen und Wagen: Sal. Oppenheim Jr. & Cie; Geschichte einer Bank und einer Familie.* München, 1989.)

TAYLOR, A. J. P. (ED.). *Bismarck: The Man and the Statesman.* New York, 1975.

URBACH, K. *Bismarck's Favorite Englishman: Lord Odo Russell's Mission.* London, 1999.

WALLER, B. *Bismarck.* Oxford, 1997.

WEGENER, W. *Naval Strategy of the World War.* Annapolis, 1989.

WEHLER, H.-U. *The German Empire, 1871–1918.* Leamington Spa, 1985. (*Das Deutsche Kaiserreich: 1871–1918.* Göttingen, 1973.)

ZEENDER J. K. *The German Center Party, 1890–1906.* Philadelphia, 1976.

INDEX

ABOUT THE AUTHOR

MICHAEL STÜRMER has been professor of history at the University of Erlangen-Nürnberg since 1973 and is currently chief correspondent for Springer-Verlag in Berlin. He has been a visiting research fellow at Harvard, the Institute for Advanced Study in Princeton, the Sorbonne, and the University of Toronto.

A NOTE ON THE TYPE

The principal text of this Modern Library edition
was set in a digitized version of Janson,
a typeface that dates from about 1690 and was cut by Nicholas Kis,
a Hungarian working in Amsterdam. The original matrices have
survived and are held by the Stempel foundry in Germany.
Hermann Zapf redesigned some of the weights and sizes for Stempel,
basing his revisions on the original design.